REFUSE TO SURRENDER

REFUSE TO SURRENDER

LESSONS IN RESILIENCE

DR. J. WILLARD KISNER

MANUSCRIPTS
PRESS

MANUSCRIPTS PRESS

COPYRIGHT © 2024 DR. J. WILLARD KISNER

REFUSE TO SURRENDER

Lessons in Resilience

ISBN   979-8-88926-092-9   *Paperback*

979-8-88926-093-6   *Hardcover*

979-8-88926-091-2   *eBook*

TABLE OF CONTENTS

Disclaimer:

The information in this book is based on my personal journey. It is not intended to replace the advice or counsel of a doctor or health professional. Each individual responds differently, and your course of treatment or diagnosis may differ from what is stated in this book. You should rely only on the advice of your physician or health professional.

A Change of Heart

Walking down a stony path
I came upon a gentle man,
"How are you this day kind sir?"
I asked as he passed my way,
curious to what he might say.

"I'm doing fine, you see,
I am coming from where you go."
He said, "Your spirit will change today
in such an amazing way."

"You have seen the outcome then,
to where this path reaches its end?"
I asked to further understand,
"What have you to tell me friend,
to ease my burden that I not bend?"

He smiled and cheerfully did say,
"Be joyful in the steps you take."
"The journey is your own, trust in yourself
believing you will be successful.
Each step you take defines your destiny."
As I continued on, I considered
the possibilities of what he said.
Where the path grew steep, in a whisper,
I heard within my thoughts,

"I am here with you, at your side.
For in every journey a lesson thrives."

--Dennis White

Introduction
-The Journey

———

Can a person control their destiny?

"If he has the will to live, and is meant to live, he will live," the doctor said. Upon my arrival in this world, I refused to die, and some sixty-eight years later, I refused to surrender to death once again. I recall that frightening day in June 2021, the day I knew I was going to die. Out of nowhere, I experienced shortness of breath. As I approached the emergency room, I became fearful and anxious, but at the same time, instinctively, my determination locked in. I refused to surrender. At first, I ignored the symptoms by rationalizing it as some minor condition. I felt certain this episode would soon pass. However, the increasing intensity and frequency of these symptoms refused to be ignored.

My story begins in the summer of 2021, when I was at a place in life to start relaxing and enjoying family and friends. The stage was set for a summer I had only dreamed of for several years. Anxious anticipation swirled around my head, thinking only of all the joys of summer that lay ahead. Later it became apparent those thoughts and feelings were mixed with early warnings of my impending demise, that I totally ignored. I didn't have any indication of how my future would be changed forever.

This game changer started on June 28, 2021. How did I know, how is this possible, how could this happen to me? I had never been hospitalized for anything other than a couple of broken bones and knee surgery, never prescribed medications, or diagnosed with any illness. I was living without limitations and with a quality of life that felt good. I could do pretty much anything I needed or wanted to do. I had no idea of what lay ahead on this journey, and I was completely unprepared. With such a clean medical history, I was naive and would soon be blindsided. I was unsuspecting with such a clean health history—incomprehensible. Note to self: just because you have a desired plan, it doesn't mean you will get what you want. Prepare for the unknown.

As the days passed, the symptoms persisted, worsening until I could no longer catch my breath—suffering intermittently with bouts of fainting and constant gasping for air. Through rationalizing it was nothing and life would soon return to normal, I fooled myself. From that memorable day, the unimaginable came to fruition. As I lay in a hospital bed from June 28, 2021 until November 19, 2021, a total of 144 days, most of my waking hours were filled with the constant rumination of thoughts: *Why me? What if? How did this happen? Why was I given more time on earth? What purpose am I to fulfill? What am I missing? Why?* Neon sign, please. Give me something, at least a clue! These questions and more inspired the writing of this book.

I wrote this book for a couple of reasons, the primary reason being for anyone facing complex long-term medical issues, mainly transplant patients. Second, I wrote this book for anyone who lost their momentum and direction in life, teetering between helpless and hopeless. Hopefully, for either reason, many will find hope and the goal to continue their journey.

This book will stimulate your mind and hug your heart. While this story is unique to me, it is relatable to many. My narrative should help those who are in need, have lost hope, or are unable to go on. I hope to increase self-awareness through the dissemination of personal stories, life's challenges related to my heart transplant and rehabilitation. I hope this book serves to build hope and resilience to cross the finish line. I hope you choose to walk with me and become a part of my journey to gain insight into your own health. I am optimistic and believe you can increase your longevity, improve the quality of your life, and conquer any challenges that lie ahead. It is up to *you!*

This book is about Faith, Hope, Endurance, which I believe equates to Resilience. Resilience is defined as the ability to adapt well in the face of adversity, trauma, threats, or multiple sources of stress, producing profound personal growth. This book is about increasing your "bounce back"—Resilience.

As a bonus, at the end of each chapter you will find a *Lesson in Resilience* to add insight to what I learned from those experiences of life. Enjoy.

Resilience,
Power of the Will, leads to
the Power of Intention, leads to
the Power of Commitment, leads to
the Power of Surrender, become self-actualized
The purpose of life is a life of purpose.

Lesson in Resilience: My journey has given me many scars, both figuratively and literally. From the literal side, the scars created from the transplant surgery. Figuratively, all the emotional scars created from the trauma of life challenges. A scar is evidence of healing, which makes the area stronger than before.

CHAPTER 1

Life Begins with Uncertainties

Do miracles exist or are they just random sequences that occur and appear miraculous?

Born December 12, 1952, six weeks premature and a bastard child, the only information on my birth certificate was "male," my mother's name, Frances M. Ellis, with the place for my father's name left blank. My name would be changed twice before I left the hospital. First, James Willard Ellis, then to James Willard Uhler, probably to conceal my illegitimacy. On the last change, a father's name was added, Bill Uhler—a man I would never meet or know. Mom, a forward thinker, knew if my name stayed Ellis, it would haunt us both for the rest of our lives. My uncles (her two brothers) were convinced my mother created the name Uhler to conceal my illegitimacy. Many years later, in 2003, at my mother's funeral, both her brothers held to the story there was not a man in her life at the time of my conception, and I was the product of a brief encounter or something more tragic.

For me, life began with uncertainties filled with lies and cover-ups to conceal the truth about my "real father." At the age of sixteen, I learned my (as I knew him) biological father, Ben Kisner, was not my biological father. Not until I was age fifty-one did I learn he only changed my last name to his name, but he never adopted me. Here's the truth: he was the only father I knew. Every inch of my being wanted him to be my real father and that is the only way I loved him, as he was my flesh and blood. This is still a mystery to me today. The answer to that question died with my mother and father, sealed away for eternity.

My mother experienced complications during her pregnancy that caused my birth to occur six weeks early. In retrospect, I suspect the burden of maintaining three jobs caused my early arrival. Plus, over the years, I learned she worried about everything and anything. She wasn't at peace if she didn't have anything to worry about; she even would call friends and worry about their problems. She was a very loving, "give it all" soul and always did the right thing. I miss her.

She kept that rigorous schedule of maintaining three jobs to provide financial support for her mom and father, who were unable to work due to health issues, and her brother Raleigh, while he attended college.

Upon delivery, I weighed in at two pounds four ounces and less than ten inches in length. At that time, medicine had not advanced to offer much assistance to preemies. In fact, according to a 2002 report by University of California at Berkley, from 1946 until the early 1980s, no babies weighing less than two pounds three ounces lived (Almond, Chay, and Lee 2002).

I made it by a slim one-ounce margin.

At the time of my birth, Mom lived at home with her parents, and I was fatherless. My grandfather stepped up and took on the additional role of being my father, what an honor for me. When I was brought home from the hospital, Granddaddy had laid an empty two-pound coffee can on its side and folded a small tea towel in the bottom. I slept on that tea towel in that can until I gained some weight and size to be able to maintain a normal body temperature. Then I was moved into a bassinet next to Nanny's bed. Several years later, Nanny told me at my birth the doctor said, "If he is meant to live, he will live." I did live and it was strictly by my will and His will. I had no clue I would hear very similar words sixty-eight years later, nor did I realize I possessed the inherent will to survive and thrive, a trait I continue to develop.

Later, I learned that due to Mom's work schedule, my breastfeeding was shortened and brought to an abrupt end. As those early years passed, I can only recall a few memories of Mom. All I wanted was to be held tight to her bosom, her arms wrapped around me, hearing her say, "I love you and miss you so much, Jimmy." I recall asking Nanny several times, "Where's Mom?" and her response was always the same, "Your mom will be home soon." Even though I was very young, I sensed a strong bond between mother and me. I felt her absence from my day-to-day life, and I yearned for her presence. All this was emotionally painful and left many scars. Later in life, these scars would show up in failed relationships that caused generational ripples.

I always found ways to cope with the pain and eventually learned ways to fill the emotional cracks left by my absent parents. I deflected most of my feelings by staying busy with activities, keeping my anguish at bay. I can recall the many times all I wanted was my mother and father. I was often asked by mean kids at school and by family members, "Jimmy, who is your father? Jimmy, how come your mother is never around? Where is your mother?"

I learned years later that Mom's work schedule took her from home for days and weeks at a time. As for my father, he didn't exist. Unbearable at times, but what made it bearable was my grandparents' unconditional love. I could always and forever count on them. They were understanding and gave their love freely and abundantly, always unconditionally. After all, I was the first grandchild. Can you spell "S-p-o-i-l-e-d?"

Think for a moment about what would happen if my grandparents weren't there to fill the gap created by absent parents. Yes, I get it, grandparents can't replace the void created from abandonment of the biological parents. What is it they say? "It sure beats nothing."

By now you're probably thinking we've made it through the worst part of my life, so we can now take a deep breath. The worst is behind me, and life will be much easier and more predictable from here on out. If only the world worked that way and was filled with certainties and guarantees. For sure, not ever, but wouldn't life be boring?

But what I've always known is His promise that He will not leave me as an orphan, and He will come to me. I have rested in peace with this my entire life. He has always kept His promise. As a result, I learned to be strong and courageous. You have to step off the boat; God can't make you.

Lesson in Resilience: Acknowledge your own reactions to uncertainty. One simple way to practice being emotionally unguarded (to build resilience) is to express to friends how much you value their friendship. Naturally, this would occur after spending time together and if you both desire to nurture the relationship and be able to express how much you admire, respect, or love this person. In a child, you can see resilience developing by how they can self-regulate, take healthy risks, willing to try again if they fail, take responsibility, and feel optimistic about outcomes.

CHAPTER 2

My First Six Years— Meet the Ellises

When you suffer with trauma, you come out on the other side either bitter or better.

My formative years living with my grandparents were cherished times. I learned many strong character traits and the importance of relationships. They instilled in me that breaking bread with loved ones makes an emotional connection. It is as essential as breathing and adds quality and significance to life. Even today when I meet with family or friends, it's over food or beverage. It is a time that brings us closer by developing a deeper understanding of the other person. As Nanny used to say in broken Italian, "Amici e famiglia, vengono a travola e mangiare" which translates to "Friends and family, come to the table and eat." Food shared with others makes the most satisfying dish.

One of those times I hold very near and dear to my heart is Uncle Joe who stopped by every morning to eat breakfast prepared by Nanny. His routine started with several cups of coffee, then he ate two slices of white bread with two basted soft eggs. I remember as I sat across the table from him to watch with fascination as he dipped his white bread (not toast) into the runny egg yolks, but he never ate the egg whites. While he ate breakfast, neighbors would pop in and out to grab coffee, eat, or just chat. But a mystery to me is that Granddaddy never joined Uncle Joe and me for breakfast. I often wondered why, but it will always remain a mystery and I will never find the answer to that question.

Raleigh Duke Ellis Sr. (12/27/1902–10/08/1963), my maternal grandfather, was a funeral director, embalmer, and furniture builder at Hill Furniture in downtown Suffolk. At night, he prepared bodies for funerals, and during the day, he built caskets and furniture and did residential carpentry, mostly flooring. He worked mornings building furniture and some afternoons he installed linoleum in homes. Granddaddy relied on a coworker for transportation to and from the remodeling work. The coworker came by the house every morning and picked him up for work and would drop off his wife to help Nanny around the house with chores and cooking. Every evening, they returned to drop off Granddaddy and his coworker picked up his wife. Since Granddaddy didn't own a car, he walked to his destinations.

Granddaddy was drafted toward the end of World War II when there was a shortage of recruits and the army was forced to recruit older men; however, Granddaddy failed the physical and wasn't allowed to fight for his country. Even though rejected by the military standard, he wanted to serve his country in some capacity. He found he could do this by working on embattled war ships in dry dock at the Norfolk shipyards. He worked there for several years, even after the war. He then worked at Planters Peanuts for a while. The factory was located at the end of the street where we lived. Granddaddy, a quiet man, always wore a smile. He was a full-blooded Irishman, which was evident by his beautiful wavy red hair and freckles on his arms.

Some Saturday mornings, I found myself sitting next to him on the front porch waiting patiently as he read the newspaper for what seemed like days for my favor part of the day. After he finished reading the paper, he wouldn't utter a sound but stood up and started walking toward downtown. That was my cue to get up and tag along. Upon our arrival at the fruit market, the clerk went over to a fifty-five-gallon barrel, lifted the lid, dipped his hand in, and grabbed a fat, juicy, sour pickle to hand to me. Then Granddaddy and I moved over to the elevated chairs for him to get his shoes shined. While eating my pickle and sitting in those elevated chairs next to him, I felt secure and reassured, as if I were on top of the world. As I reflect on those times, I can honestly say I don't remember Granddaddy ever uttering a word. I remember people came and sat next to him, but they only whispered into each other's ears when speaking. Granddaddy was a stoic man. However, the only side I ever knew was tender, gentle, and loving.

Clara Marie Edwards Ellis (10/13/1900–03/23/1972), was my maternal grandmother, whom I called Nanny. Nanny and Granddaddy were married in 1933 and remained so until Granddaddy's death in 1963. Nanny always said she wanted to live long enough to see her first grandchild graduate from high school. God granted her wish. Nanny lived until 1972, ten months after I graduated from high school. I often wonder why she didn't ask to live until her great-grandchild graduated from high school.

After Nanny and Granddaddy married, they produced four offspring: Aunt Elizabeth, Uncle Raleigh Jr., Uncle Joe, and Frances Marie. After raising four children, Nanny went to work for an awning company. She sewed awnings and tents. Uncle Joe worked for the same company. He installed awnings, tents, and storm windows on residential and commercial buildings. I remember the times I went to work with Nanny. On each corner of the large sewing tables that seemed as large as a football field sat a sewing machine; Nanny worked at one of those. To occupy my time while Nanny worked, Uncle Joe made a swing and suspended it from the ceiling in the center of one of those tables. I would swing above the table while Nanny sewed.

Nanny's health started declining at an early age when she was first diagnosed with diabetes. The disease had greatly diminished her vision and overall health. At that time, we didn't know much about diabetes or how to control it. As a result, Nanny suffered with the many medical complications associated with being a very large person. She also developed cataracts early in life, but they weren't removed until many years later. Her vision worsened, leaving her legally blind. She couldn't see to drive. No matter the circumstances, even without her vision and the many additional medical issues, she never complained or felt sorry for herself. With all these issues stacked against her, she was still grateful to have her family, her faith, and the ability to sew awnings, crochet, and knit—all by feel.

Nanny, a spirit-filled, devoted Christian, committed her life as a soldier in the Salvation Army. Whenever she attended a church service or function, she dressed in full uniform, including the bonnet. At Christmas time, she could be found at one of the entrances of a department store in full uniform, with the little red hanging kettle, ringing the bell for donations. At times, she was too ill and weak to stand, but she went anyway. They would bring a chair for her to sit so she could continue her mission. Nanny was by far a remarkable human being. I am so blessed she was a big foundational piece forming my character, my belief system, and my tender heart.

On some of those mornings following breakfast, depending on Nanny's energy level and desirable weather, she and I walked two blocks to downtown Suffolk to shop. Nanny loved to shop even though most times she returned home empty-handed. Most of those walks took upward of two hours. *Why?* you ask. If you knew Nanny and the folks who lived in our neighborhood, you would know the answer. Our neighborhood was composed of row housing, which meant the houses were spaced six feet apart. Starting with the house we lived in at the other end of the block and going toward downtown Suffolk, our street had eight houses on each side. As we walked toward downtown without encountering interaction, Nanny became distraught when her social quotient was not being replenished.

Then she would look across the street to see if more people were outside. If so, she hurriedly grabbed my hand as we dashed across the street to the other side in hopes that someone would be a willing participant. Some days were better than others. If everyone was outside and she talked to each person for a minimum of fifteen minutes, there went two hours. Nanny was prosocial with a strong desire to connect and share her love with everyone she spoke to.

In Nanny's world, strangers didn't exist. I would at times observe as she immersed herself in the affairs and details of her neighbors' lives, being fully attentive in every word. I kept occupied by exploring the surrounding area in minute detail, all the while focused on advancing toward our destination. When we finally made it to town, we'd window-shop and examine every piece of merchandise in the store by going down every aisle. At the end of our shopping adventure, we almost always came home empty-handed. Still today, Nanny is the only person I've known who can shop all day and not make a single purchase. This is amazing to me.

My grandparents should have been labeled "minimalists" because they didn't care about accumulating wealth or material possessions. They had no interest in buying or owning a home but instead chose to rent. They lived in the same rented home from the 1930s until 1968. The dining room served as Nanny's converted bedroom. Nanny slept on the main floor because she was unable to safely climb the stairs, and the only bathroom was on the main floor. I didn't have my own bedroom, so I alternated nights sleeping with Granddaddy and Nanny.

On the nights I slept with Nanny, prior to going to sleep, I would sit on her belly as she rocked in the rocking chair. She read scriptures from the Bible and sang hymns I loved crawling onto her feather mattress and sinking into her safe, warm, and secure arms. Granddaddy slept in an upstairs bedroom. On the nights with Granddaddy, the sound of Alka-Seltzer fizzing greeted me. I still remember the bubbles tickling my nose as I peered into the glass.

Some mornings, I'd watch Granddaddy carefully reach into the dresser drawers filled with laundered and pressed work uniforms of assorted colors. I would watch him pull out a matching shirt and pair of pants for work. Some nights, in the heat of the summer when it was too hot to sleep upstairs in the bedroom, we would bring a blanket and sleep on the back porch. While I was terrified to fall asleep outside on an open porch, Granddaddy always went right to sleep and started snoring; I became hyper-vigilant for the arrival of the boogeyman. Oh, the mighty power of fear when coupled with the imagination of a child and the unknown!

Imagine from a minimalist perspective being an adult and not owning a car. Every time you needed to go somewhere, you had to walk or hitch a ride. Incomprehensible, right? My grandparents didn't own a car until 1956, when they purchased their first automobile. You're asking why didn't they own a car before then? Because of medical expenses, they never had enough money until then. I remember that car vividly. It was a 1952 shiny black Chrysler Windsor DeLuxe. Every Saturday, Granddaddy drove the car around to the back of the house to wash and hand buff the finish to a showroom shine. He cleaned the interior and wiped all the surfaces in preparation for our Sunday outings.

On Sundays after church, Nanny and I loaded up in the back seat of the freshly cleaned car, and Granddaddy drove us to

North Carolina to Aunt Callie and Uncle Eldon's farm for a fabulous home-cooked dinner. They always prepared an enormous, made-from-scratch meal of breads, roast, ham, sweet potatoes, corn, lima beans, scalloped potatoes, and luscious desserts. After dinner, we'd retire to the swing on the screened-in front porch where I had the pleasure of listening to family stories. I found myself hanging on to every word, totally captivated. Sometimes, their son, Buddy Jones, his wife, and daughter came for dinner. Their daughter was my age. She was a slender, beautiful, sweet, and precious blond-haired little girl, my first love. In the front yard of the farmhouse was a playhouse and sandbox. We played and ran carefree for most of the afternoon. Some of my most memorable times were during those Sunday dinners.

They also instilled in me that music and song develop an emotional connection and adds significance to life. Often on Friday nights, my grandparents' home became the gathering place for people with musical talent who wanted an audience for their picking and jamming sessions. The shindig lasted into the wee hours of the morning. I contributed by mimicking Elvis Presley's dance moves and playing a guitar.

Before I was born, every Saturday morning Uncle Joe, Mom, Peewee, and other singers walked downtown to the local radio station WLPM where they played and sang live music. The call letters WLPM stood for World's Largest Peanut Market and the studio was located above the Russell Drug Store and Soda Fountain in Suffolk. Following the radio talent show, they were rewarded with movie tickets. Then they walked across the street to watch the Saturday matinee movie.

Later in life, I was able to ascertain the valuable core traits I learned in my first six years of life while with my grandparents. They were such nurturers, that gave me the security I needed for being grounded and confident. They taught me the strength of emotional connection through music and breaking bread that involves conversation. I learned the importance of a strong work ethic, knowing the importance of responsibility and accountability: "Your word is your bond." My grandparents taught me the value of family first and to always side with family. Also, attach to people and relationships not objectives or things, as those are temporary. Last, Nanny taught me to thank God in every situation; He knows the big picture, give it all to Him. My first six years gave me the building blocks for a strong foundation. Thank you, Nanny and Granddaddy. Love you and miss you.

Lesson in Resilience: Sensitivity is essential to basic human qualities that lends to the ability to feel things at a very visceral level. If sensitivity is acquired, attentional awareness is a natural tendency based on this ability of sensing heartfelt emotions, in turn building resilience.

CHAPTER 3

Gaining Hope Amid Loss

———

The losses in my life defined me, but with every loss, I learned and gained hope.

When I was around four, Mom popped up again in my life along with a man she introduced to me as my father. That was a shock, and a puzzlement to me: My father? I remember I never questioned the validity since I was without a father. I was excited to embrace this new person as my own and not question all the years he was absent. Ben A. Kisner and my mom were married by a justice of the peace in the latter part of 1956. Soon after, Mom announced she was pregnant with my brother Stuart, who was born on March 1, 1957, in Suffolk, Virginia. Shortly after Stuart's birth, my father left Suffolk to take a new job in Kansas City. The plan was for Mom and me to move to Kansas City when Stuart was stable and able to travel.

However, within a couple of days of his birth, Stuart developed a rash on his back and neck. Mom applied powder, but the rash continued to worsen. Stuart cried continuously and the powder provided no relief. Over the next twenty-four hours, Stuart's crying continued. This only increased my anxiety. Anxiety laced with fear surged through my body. Finally, Mom broke down and couldn't take Stuart's suffering any longer, so she put us both in the car and drove to the emergency room. I sensed something was seriously wrong. After the doctor examined Stuart, I heard him tell Mom the rash on his back and neck was nothing more than a heat rash and there was nothing to worry about. He instructed Mom to take Stuart home and continue what she had been doing.

After returning home, Stuart cried incessantly. Wherever I moved to in the house only amplified his cries and increased my anxiety and fear. I felt helpless, scared. I felt pain throughout my body, knowing there was nothing I could do to ease his pain. At one point, I felt my heart pulsating throughout my entire body. The only possible way for me to get any relief from the pain was to run, run as hard and as fast and as long as I could. Then I thought, *If I did run, what would happen to Stuart?* I continued to think, *I can't run, I need to stay and take care of Stuart. What if something happened to him while I was gone? Who would comfort Mom?* Over those next twenty-four hours, more thoughts than you can imagine raced through my head. *Why does he have to suffer? Whatever did he do to deserve this? Why doesn't Mom do something to make him okay?* As I write this piece of my history, I now realize as a little boy I was far too young and innocent, and this was way too much for me to process and internalize. I felt I was in this by myself, alone—way, way, too much. How did I have the courage to endure this?

The next morning, Stuart's cry was silenced. I figured now he was okay. But suddenly, Mom hurriedly loaded Stuart and me in the car and drove to the emergency room. Upon our arrival, Mom explained to the nurse Stuart had cried continuously for the last twenty-four hours and the rash continued to worsen, but suddenly, he stopped crying. The nurse abruptly took him out of Mom's arms and placed him on a bed and wheeled him away. Mom ran alongside the bed as they went into a room and closed the door. Once again, I was left behind. In the waiting room, I was alone and afraid of what might happen next. After a while, Mom came out from the room crying. She came over to where I was sitting and reached out to grab my hand to take me back to Stuart's room.

Mom used the phone in the room to call my father to tell him the urgency of the matter with Stuart. I heard her say the words, "Stuart is not going to make it." I instantly froze, she went on to say to Father, "You must come home as soon as possible." When she hung up the phone, she said Father would be back in Suffolk in about seventeen hours.

Soon the doctor came into the room to tell Mom that Stuart's body temperature was 106.5 degrees. He was diagnosed with hyperpyrexia. According to WebMD, "hyperpyrexia is a condition where the body temperature goes above 106.7 degrees Fahrenheit (41.5 degrees Celsius) due to changes in the hypothalamus—the organ in the brain that regulates temperature" (2023). If it progresses, it ultimately leads to organ failure and death.

The last resort was to pack him in ice to lower his body temperature. Mom and I left the room and went back to the waiting room. After they completed this drastic procedure, we were allowed back in the room to be with Stuart only to see him lying in a tub filled with ice packed around him. Seeing him this way petrified me. It left an indelible impression that haunts my memory still today. Mom continued to cry and had not stopped crying since arriving at the emergency room.

I was confused about all of this and wondered if I should cry or what. I was so young and innocent, asking myself what this all meant since I was not given any explanation. All those negative thoughts ran through my head. *Why is this happening to Stuart? He is only a baby. Babies only cry when they are tired, hungry, or in pain? Why is Mom crying? Surely Stuart is going to be okay, isn't he?* I now know I didn't have the experience to understand anything about pain or dying. After all, I had only experienced joy and happiness in my life. I couldn't make any sense of what was occurring with Stuart lying there lifeless, void of emotions. I remembered how frightened and lonely I felt but not a clue on where and when all this would end. I knew for certain in my heart and thinking they were only hurting him more.

Mom and I continued to wait patiently for what seemed like days, but only several hours waiting for a miracle. The nurse returned to the room to check Stuart's temperature again only to report no change. I wanted to believe Stuart was in a peaceful sleep, and I would be reassured when he woke that everything would be okay. I compartmentalized that everything else occurring around me was just an insane nightmare. I kept saying to myself, "He will be okay."

After a while, the doctor returned and told Mom the doctors could not do anything more. The doctor also mentioned if the high fever continued, there was a high probability Stuart would remain in a vegetative state resulting in extensive brain damage. What did all that mean? Late that night, Father arrived after driving seventeen hours straight from Kansas City. The doctor met with my father to bring him current on Stuart's status and prognosis. When the doctor left the room, Father turned to Mom and they embraced, crying, while I stood off to the side, alone again, observing them. Stuart lay across the room, wrapped in ice—his body still and lifeless. This all seemed like a nightmare. After all, what did a four-year-old know about nightmares? I quickly learned. Father took me home and put me in bed with Nanny where I once again felt secure and safe.

The next morning, Nanny allowed me to go to the city park to play. After several hours of hard play, I heard my name being called, "Jimmy, Jimmy." I looked around and on the street corner was the priest waving his arm for me to come to him. I remember the sudden rush of emotions coming over me, so I held my breath and hesitated for a moment, bracing for the words I didn't want to hear. I felt rumbling in my belly and a sense of impending doom. As I ran toward the priest, my only thought was I didn't want to hear anything else had gone wrong. I just wanted everything to go back to the way it was last week. I wanted everything to be all right. When I got within reach of the priest, he said, "Your mother and father want you to come home."

As we approached the house, the priest pressed his hand into my back, propelling me forward. Every time he pushed, my hesitancy increased, and I pushed back and the slower my steps became. When I finally reached the front steps to the house, my fear and anxiety spun out of control, and with every step forward it was as if I were standing still, frozen. As I walked through the front door into the living room, I could hear crying and a low chatter of conversation. I looked in the direction of the chatter and activity and saw people circled around Nanny's bed. Instantly, it felt as if my heart stopped beating and my first thought was something happened to Nanny. I froze in my tracks for a second, and suddenly, I felt the giant hand of the priest pushing me forward again. As I approached Nanny's bed, the circle of people opened to allow me passage onto the bed.

Both Mom and Father were lying on the bed crying. Suddenly, I was lifted onto the bed next to them. Mom said, "Jimmy, Stuart died this morning." I felt such a surge of emotional shock; he was only seven days old (March 01, 1957–March 08, 1957). That surge of emotions catapulted me off the bed and onto the floor. I was in a dead run through the house, out the back door, and into the backyard until I reached my fort. The fort was a place of safety and security. Once inside, I fell to the ground on my knees and burst into tears.

The death of Stuart was my first experience with loss. I learned early in life that men didn't show emotions, especially not with tears. I remember the confusion I experienced over Stuart's death. At his funeral, I cried uncontrollably until my uncle who was sitting next to me hit me on the knee, telling me to stop crying because men don't cry. Suddenly I stopped crying and never cried again for some fifteen years, and then not again for thirty-one years.

Over the years, I've sought to learn to listen to my introspective voice and to have a keen self-awareness of any experiences of discovery about grief and loss. I now know authentic men can cry if they want. With the sudden death of Stuart, our plans to leave for Kansas City were postponed. After the funeral, mother couldn't cope with all the tragedies occurring in her life, which resulted in a nervous breakdown and her being hospitalized for a month or so. She wasn't prepared to grieve the loss of her new baby and being torn from the only family she knew, plus moving halfway across the country. It was obviously too much for her to bear, overwhelming to say the least.

I can still remember the debilitating fear that came over me when I realized I was moving away from the only family I had known. This move would add another loss notch onto my heart. No matter the reason for the move, I was frightened and didn't have a clue who would watch over me wherever we were headed. I couldn't comprehend the actual distance I would be away, other than I was told, "far, far away," "almost to the other side of the United States." All I could think about was, *How will I know to get back here, if I get lost?* The reason for being uprooted from our peaceful existence in Virginia was a job opportunity for my father, a man I didn't know. I didn't know him but had to trust my mother, with whom I really didn't have a tight bond. Certain uncertainties were swirling in my head. Father's brother-in-law was a professional driver and knew of several jobs for my father if we relocated to the Midwest. Since I was only a little over four when Stuart passed, I wasn't given an option to stay but to go.

Lesson in Resilience: Control your thoughts, control your emotions: you choose your thoughts; your emotions are not your thoughts. Become the victim or victor—make your thoughts positive—positive self-talk. It is important to realize that many people will come into our life for primarily a season and a few people for a lifetime. Gain resilience when you learn to thrive, despite intermittent struggles and uncertainty.

CHAPTER 4

Meet the Kisners

Blended Family = Coping with Sacrifice

Benonie Augusta Kisner (06/20/1932–04/25/2021), known to me as Father, was born in Butler, Missouri, a small town sixty miles southeast of Kansas City. He was drafted into the Navy during the Korean War. During his tour of duty, he served as a boiler operator deep in the bowels of the aircraft carrier USS Valley Forge stationed at the Norfolk, Virginia shipyards. He operated the coal-fired boilers that powered the ship. All the steam pipes that ran from the boiler were wrapped with asbestos insulation. When a pipe needed repair, he removed the insulation to make the repair. Some fifty years later, he developed mesothelioma, which required a tracheotomy. He struggled with breathing along with a couple of code blues over the years.

When he completed his obligation to the military, he again returned to the Norfolk shipyards. As soon as he hit solid ground to start his new life, he took the first available work as a truck driver for a logging company, hauling logs down the Appalachian Mountains in the Carolinas. He drove a logging truck filled with stacked logs, up and down the mountains on temporary man-made roads that were narrower than the wheelbase of the trailer. My father quickly learned of the dangerous nature of driving the logging truck; it was only a matter of time before a serious accident might occur. The hourly pay for driving these trucks was too low and could not provide the financial support necessary to sustain the quality of life for his family. Therefore, he made a change and took a job with Safeway Grocery as a driver hauling produce from California to Kansas City. In the interim, he met my mom while she was working at one of her jobs in Norfolk. After they dated for a while, he proposed and they were married at the home of the justice of the peace in 1956, in Suffolk, Virginia.

He was a farm boy, and his roots ran deep in the Midwest; he yearned to return home to the Midwest for the air, four seasons, and family.

For me, the trip to Kansas City was long and agonizing, especially so soon after the death of Stuart and leaving behind Nanny and Granddaddy, two people who had loved me so deeply and to whom I was so bonded.

When Mom and I arrived in Kansas City, we moved in with my father's mother, grandmother Violet Mariam Eddy Kisner (December 09, 1895–November 25, 1959). She lived on the first floor of a two-story flat she owned, while renters occupied the second floor. Grandmother Violet didn't own a car and preferred to travel by trolley or bus if available. Whenever she and I ventured out of the house, she pulled around a two-wheeled metal cart to hold whatever goods we gathered on our journey.

Since my father was an over-the-road truck driver for Safeway, he was gone two to three weeks a month. I remember shortly after moving in with grandmother Violet when father came home for the first time. He came through the door carrying a package he handed to me to open. It was a model airplane he and I later assembled. After living there for several months, he brought me a basic train set on one of his returns from the road. In the basement, father had built a table for the train set to be installed. Over the next weeks and months, he continued bringing home additions to the train set that expanded our landscaping terrain and distance for the train to travel. After a while, we added bridges, more towns with train depots, and beautiful, realistic landscaping. It felt so real, especially when I rested my chin on the table, placing my eyes level with the train. Those were awesome times and very fond memories.

It seemed like only a short time before my parents experienced marital discord. I thought the primary cause of conflict was due to the current living arrangement, but as I reflect on it, all the reasons for marital problems were present—the death of Stuart, Mom being transplanted some eleven hundred miles away from her family, and she wasn't allowed to phone her family because of his jealously and the expense of long-distance calls. This changed her life forever. Her only mode of communication was (snail) mail. Mom, faithfully, wrote her parents weekly, and her parents wrote back to her weekly. I also received a weekly letter from Nanny, which included two dimes taped to the top of the letter. Today I hold those cherished letters close to my heart.

The losses and the stress of moving halfway across the country not only affected mother deeply, emotionally and physically, but now had affected me. I developed symptoms of stomach cramping, regurgitation, passing blood, and bowel inconsistency. I had developed peptic (gastric) ulcers. The testing and treatment were more traumatic than all my life experiences thus far. The stress of a combination of everything in my life so far was weighing a heavy toll on my spirit, both physical and emotional.

Pretty soon, Mom and I returned to Virginia. After settling back in with Nanny and Granddaddy, Mom vaporized again. I didn't see much of her, but it was a good trade-off. I was content and overflowing with joy being back with my grandparents.

Soon after returning to Virginia, I started first grade. One day after school, I went next door to play with the neighbor boy, Roger. He had a croquet mallet and a couple of toys he no longer wanted. He wanted my toys instead, so he took them. I didn't want to give him my toys, so I took them back. He didn't like that, so he picked up his mallet and hit me on the top of my forehead. It started bleeding profusely. I ran home crying. My uncles were there visiting Granddaddy and Nanny at the time. When I came into the house crying and bleeding, both uncles quickly ran next door to find little Roger. I was loaded into the car and taken to the hospital where I received seven stitches. I didn't think it was a big deal but everyone else seemed very upset, especially Nanny. Later, I learned that Uncle Joe went into Roger's house and found him hiding under his bed. Uncle Joe dragged Roger outside, spanking him all the way to the backyard.

During the middle of my first-grade school year, circumstances changed, and we returned to Kansas City. By now most of my ulcer symptoms had gone into remission, but what now? We moved in with grandmother Violet again. She died shortly after we had moved in. Our future existence was up in the air and undecided. All I needed was more uncertainty in my life.

While we stayed there, I made friends with some of the neighbors, the Gaineys. They were a large family—three girls and two boys. Mr. Gainey was a fire chief in Kansas City. As a second job, he sold insurance for State Farm Insurance Company. I spent a lot of time with the Gaineys. Sometimes we made trips to the fire station. I played with the fire station dalmatian. I got to ride on the fire truck when they were running errands or taking short trips. I also went with Mr. Gainey when he made house calls selling insurance. He was a dynamic individual, a powerful, fun man, and a practical joker. One time while in their home, one of Mr. Gainey's sons took off my tennis shoes, and then my socks, and then placed my foot up to his nose. He sniffed my feet and made a stinky sound. From then on he called me *Stinky Feet*. It drove me crazy. I was spoiled being around the three girls and two boys. They were teenagers and young adults at the time.

I remember another time when I was playing in the front yard of grandmother Kisner's home, a camera man came by with a pony trying to sell photos. He convinced Mom to purchase a photo. I dressed in full cowboy gear that the photographer provided. He sat me on the pony, dressed like a cowboy so he could take a goofy picture.

On another occasion, Father and I were outside doing yard work and throwing around a ball playing catch when he fell to the ground. I first thought he was joking around, but he couldn't move—totally paralyzed. I started yelling for Mom because Father couldn't talk. Someone called the ambulance, and they rushed him to the hospital. He was diagnosed with polio and placed in an iron lung. He was paralyzed for a short time. Miraculously, following an extended stay, he was released from the hospital with no permanent paralysis or limitations.

Sometime in March of 1958, we packed our belongings and moved to a farm in Lenexa, Kansas. The farm was in the middle of nowhere. The closest house was two and a half miles away, but our house was only 150 yards from an active railroad track. If those numbers could be reversed, I would have been a happy camper. The acreage surrounding the house was endless. My father was gone over the road trucking most of the time and my mom and I were left in this desolate area to fend for ourselves. Mom was pregnant and was expected to deliver in June of 1958.

While Father and Mom were at the hospital delivering my younger brother Scott, I was left at home to attend school. I was enrolled in the second grade. Before Mom left for the hospital, she instructed me to ride the bus home from school and Mr. Hebb, our closest neighbor, would pick me up in the driveway. After school, the bus dropped me off at our driveway, but no one was there to pick me up. I walked around to the back door of the house, but the door was missing. It was lying on the floor inside the house.

My first thought was, *Father must have forgotten his key and had to break down the door to get in.* Everything was thrown out of the drawers and onto the floor. I thought my dad couldn't find something. I was disturbed and confused about what happened. Mr. Hebb showed up and took me to his house. I was told the house had been robbed, and I missed the robbers by only a few minutes. If the bus had been a little bit earlier, I might not be writing this story now. The robbers stole my dad's gun collection, coin collection, and his new Sears tool chest, which was filled with tools.

We remained on the farm until early 1960 after the break-in and near miss. With Father's job requiring him to be on the road for weeks at a time, Mom was too afraid to stay there with a newborn. She did stick with her original promise of staying for two years. My father was also able to accomplish his goal of becoming totally self-sufficient. The purchase of a milk cow, feeder calves, a chicken for laying eggs, and a pig helped him achieve his goal.

He also planted a garden and a strawberry patch and bought a butter churn. My father churned butter, Mom canned yams, corn, green beans, and even meat. When Father butchered a cow, he insisted we utilize the entire animal. We prepared meals from every part of the animal, and I do mean every part of the animal—the tongue and brain—anything else the cow produced. The pig produced pickled pig's feet and cured ham.

One time, Father bought 150 chicks for us to raise. Once they grew to the right size, he invited my aunts and cousins to help prepare them for freezing. We cleaned, bagged, and prepared those chickens and put them in the freezer. That time on the farm was wonderful, fulfilling, and awakening, and something most people will never have an opportunity to experience. I wish it could have continued.

Next, we moved to Independence, Missouri, the home of Harry S. Truman, our thirty-third president of the United States. We rented a house on Kings Highway with two bedrooms, one bath, and a detached garage. In June of 1960, my third brother, Brett, was born. Scott, Brett, and I grew up in that house. Three growing boys shared a cozy existence in a single bedroom, for several years. In 1966, my parents built a new home a block down the street. My parents lived in Independence until their deaths.

Back in Suffolk, Virginia, in 1962, Granddaddy and Nanny purchased a building across the street from their home and opened Ellis Grocery. That next summer, I took a train alone to Virginia to spend the summer with my grandparents. The train ride took about two days. When I arrived in Suffolk, I heard the conductor announcing our arrival over the loudspeakers, "Now arriving at Suffolk, Virginia." I really got excited and knew for sure I was home, especially when I saw Uncle Joe walking toward me.

We loaded into his work truck and drove to my grandparents' store. As soon as Uncle Joe stopped the truck, I jumped out and ran into the store, hugging them both so hard they each let out a big groan. I felt like I was in the middle of a beautiful dream that I was finally home. When we'd left Virginia about three years earlier, I honestly thought I'd never see them again. That night, Nanny fixed a big old Southern dinner of comfort food—fried chicken, black-eyed peas, mashed potatoes, and fried cornbread, and of course banana pudding. I was in heaven.

Knowing I would return to Independence at the end of the summer, I already had regrets. It seemed I was at the grocery store all my waking hours. The days were long as the store was open twelve hours a day except on Sunday. My entire summer existed at the grocery store, and I loved every minute of it. People would come in, and I listened to them as they talked about the latest gossip and told stories from the past.

Sometimes I assisted the ladies by taking the items they wanted off the shelves and placing them into my cart. Other times, customers would phone in their orders. I would fill them and deliver them to their homes in my wagon and write out a receipt. Upon my return, Nanny rewarded me with chocolate milk or candy.

I have many fond memories of working at the Ellis Grocery store.

In 1963, we lost Granddaddy.

It all happened while Granddaddy and Nanny were at their store. Granddaddy was sitting in the back room on his bar stool when he suddenly lost consciousness, causing him to fall backward onto the floor. Nanny heard the noise and went to the back of the store to find Granddaddy lying motionless. He didn't have a pulse and wasn't breathing. She called for the paramedics. When they arrived, they found a nitroglycerin pill under his tongue. They worked to revive Granddaddy for over an hour and a half at a grueling pace.

They were unable to resuscitate him. They transported Granddaddy to the hospital and kept him on life support, but he was still flatlined and they pronounced him DOA. Nanny later learned from his doctor that Granddaddy had congestive heart failure. The doctor had prescribed the nitroglycerin pills to keep his heart beating; however, Granddaddy never told anyone.

The years I spent living and learning from my grandparents I can honestly say were the best years of my life. What did those years teach me? Those years taught me survival, the importance of family, and to make everyone you meet your friend. They taught me the connecting power of food; the endurance of my will, tenacity/intention, and never-say-die spirit; and the importance of finishing well, but most importantly finish with dignity and respect of others.

Lesson in Resilience: Remain open to new ideas that will expand your vast horizons. Always be open to seeking help from others when uncertain and unsure. The key is to master the challenge, and it's okay to ask for guidance or help.

CHAPTER 5

Graduation

———

According to Merriam-Webster's dictionary, one meaning of the term "graduation" is "the award or acceptance of an academic degree or diploma."

I lived in Independence, Missouri until the twelfth grade, when I graduated from high school. I grew up with the belief "my body's a temple"—respect it and take care of it, and it will take care of you.

I remember around age twelve, I became more curious about the people who were my neighbors. I started venturing out, walking down the street until I found someone outside, (sound familiar) then I would approach them to start a conversation. On one of those outings, I found a neighbor who was lifting weights in his garage. I stayed and talked with him during his entire workout. As a result, he invited me to start working out with him every evening after dinner. After dinner the following night and many to follow, I would run across the street to the neighbor's house to learn how to lift weights, the different muscle groups, and how to build muscle.

Later that summer, I met a guy who played on the scrimmage squad for the Kansas City Chiefs football team. The Chiefs worked out at the European Health Spa on Highway 40 in

Independence, Missouri. He invited me to join him for some workouts and was able to get me a free pass for a couple of weeks. I asked my parents for an early birthday present: a membership to the health club. They ended up buying me a lifetime membership. I was able to work out daily. He knew everything about exercise and nutrition.

He taught me about the many benefits of protein and nutritional supplements. I was drinking protein shakes before they hit the retail market. My protein shakes consisted of two cups of whole milk, three packets of Knox gelatin (protein), two cracked eggs, and fresh fruit. Mom took the Knox gelatin to strengthen her nails. She would go into the pantry to grab a packet and find an empty box. She reminded me several times not to take her packets of gelatin but to buy my own. Those were the days—many, many, fond memories. He taught me much about healthy eating and protein-enriched diets. The information I learned helped this skinny kid gain weight and muscle mass.

During my senior year of high school, my father and I collided with irreconcilable differences, and my only choice was to move out of the family home. Since I was working nights cleaning offices and the shop at Jerry Hayes Ford dealership, I could afford my own apartment. I didn't have a choice: he controlled my every move, what I ate, what I wore, who my friends were, etc. Finally I could experience some breathing room.

I graduated from high school in 1971, amid the final chaos of the Vietnam War. I remember receiving a military draft letter requesting me to report for a physical and induction.

Upon receipt of this letter, I had to decide whether to attend college or to serve my country in Vietnam. I had already lost three neighborhood friends to this hideous war and was convinced I would be number four if I opted for a tour of duty. My decision was to attend college until my father decided differently. My decision was heavily influenced by my father's ridicule. Through this experience, I decided to man up and report for duty. The morning I reported for my physical was the most frightening day of my life. I could not stop the shaking and cold sweat.

After completing the induction process, I was told I would receive a decision letter within a few days. For those several days and nights, I agonized over that letter. I couldn't sleep, and I had no appetite. My thoughts were filled with nightmares of war and death. Finally, I received the letter from the military. It stated I had failed my physical because of a bad knee. During my sophomore year of high school football, I had torn my meniscus and required surgery. Since I failed the physical, my only option was to attend college. Father never forgave me for not going to war.

I didn't understand at the time, but it seemed my father had not prioritized, as I had, my going to college and playing football. It is obvious to me now: the direction he wanted me to go—either military or find a career. Now I understand why Chick Wheeler, was head of operations at the Ford Motor Plant, who got me a job (without my inquiring) after graduation, hanging bumpers. Father had his own agenda. Sneaky! My career at Ford was short lived, only lasting 5 days. I knew for sure I was college bound.

Before being confronted with the option of going to war, I had planned to attend college and play football. Several college recruiters approached me with offers that made college a financially attainable dream. When I received the rejection notice from the military, it was difficult for me to accept that my life was spared. Once again, I would be able to attend college. However, before that could happen, I had to make several convincing phone calls to college recruiters to explain the sudden shift of direction. In August of 1971, I reported for football camp at Missouri Western College and signed on to play football, a sport at which I truly excelled. I must come clean; my first love was baseball, but because of the injury to my right knee (as a pitcher, my pivotal knee) I was not a contender at the college level.

I was awarded a full-ride football scholarship. However, I did not understand the scholastic responsibility tied to that scholarship. My primary academic goal was to become a medical doctor. I came prepared to excel in football and participate fully in all extracurricular activities. I embraced the entitlement and prestige that came with playing football. Unfortunately, I only embraced and excelled at all the extracurricular activities.

My parents did not have the knowledge or foresight to understand the benefits of attending college. In fact, they had me convinced I needed to pursue a "practical profession." Therefore, I chose to pursue a degree in business. During my first semester of school, I took a psychology course and experienced an immediate fondness for both the subject and the professor, Willis H. McCann, PhD. We spent many hours over dinner discussing life and psychology. While I didn't have much knowledge of either subject, I had a thirst and desire to learn, especially if someone was willing to mentor me.

During my second year of school, I met the girl of my dreams. My focus soon turned from football and partying to finding a career and marriage. I left college after two and half years and didn't return for twelve. I married Denise Marie Grill on May 4, 1974. It was not long before the marriage became severed. I carried many scars, unrealistic expectations, and the childhood baggage that left me with generational ripples in my relationship. I harbored deep, unsettling guilt for not completing my college education and losing my athletic scholarship.

I married a woman who was deeply in love and devoted to me, and for whom I thought I had that same love. Her expectation of me was to guide our relationship. Unbeknownst to me, I was not ready to accept that level of responsibility that required deep-seated emotions on my side. What constantly nagged at me was furthering my education. I saw college slipping away and becoming a distant memory replaced by the many challenges of trying to be a husband and becoming a father. It takes two people to form a relationship but only one person to destroy the relationship. I single-handedly destroyed a beautiful relationship. The fatality of living blind and self-absorbed. If I knew then what I know today— hindsight can be a curse.

Because I had attended two years of college, played my favorite sport, and was clear on how I was to achieve my goals, I felt prepared for life. Indeed, I thought everything I had accomplished was the pinnacle of what life is all about—working hard, raising a family, and owning material things, when, in fact, I was living under false pretenses and blinded by the lies.

I came to realize I did not know nearly as much as I believed I knew about responsibilities and relationships. I eventually learned life throws hard balls and curve balls. I would eventually learn to hit those out of the park. However, I gained the most knowledge and wisdom through formal education. My marriage suffered for many years because my focus was on career and social status. The beliefs and patterns instilled by my family and the abandonment of my birth father created a huge void inside of me, resulting in tremendous self-doubt and unrest. For many years, I tried to find substantive value in relationships and objectives to fill that void in my life. Regardless of how hard I searched to fill that void with worthless, meaningless relationships and big-boy toys, I struggled with being cut off from my emotions and unable to experience fulfillment in my marriage or in other ways.

For many years, I lived filled with fear, anxiety, and worry, unable to focus on one thing long enough to establish any routine or long-term vision for my life. The more this became apparent, the more meaningless life became. I was constantly attempting to grab anything that gave me instant gratification as I continued to flounder and fumble through life.

I began questioning every aspect of my life, creating more self doubt. As I tried to make life corrections and adjust my course, I found my focus narrowed my options, and the calmer and more focused I became. Things in my life slowed down and stopped spiraling out of control.

The more I developed goals and set my commitments, the more my intentions grew, thus, my focus intensified. Fighting against the fight, flight, or freeze response, my vision began clearing. As I began to mature and slow down, life started to take shape in an ascent direction. I started formulating an internal mission and purpose dialogue. Even though my life was experiencing a transformation, the deep-seated issues present caused an inability to handle a long-term, committed relationship.

By now you're shaking your head in amazement or asking yourself, "Did everything up to this point really happen to one person?" Just think what you have read so far are just snippets of my first twenty-something years. Those years of experiences defined my direction and focus and how I got to where I am today. There is much, much, more to my story, probably enough to fill the pages of another book.

Isn't life so magnificent that despite our faults and our past we are able to live every breath to the fullest? As I reflect on my early childhood, I recognize that I started out as though I was figuratively hanging on by my fingertips, dangling from a cliff, wondering why I was the exception. Why was I given life? Questions I would again ask myself some sixty-eight years later. This stark beginning allowed me to fight the good fight, and I was able to hold on to life and thrive. I can remember many times reminiscing about my past, finding myself blinking back the tears but continuing to forge ahead with life. One could argue the deck was stacked against me, but I played the cards dealt and fought against the odds. It is with certainty that I know there are people who have it rougher and tougher than my story. I know each of us possesses the strength and tenacity to develop the will that fuels our determination to finish the race.

> ***Lesson in Resilience:*** The capacity to recover quickly from difficulties. Life is tough. If you are moving forward, you will have challenges—get used to it. Ride the big wave for as long as you can before reaching shore. Remember overcoming challenges produces resilience, gaining endurance makes it easier next time. Let that soak in.

CHAPTER 6

The Harsh Jolt of Reality—Staying Alive

Fast forward some forty-three years to June 28, 2021, my expiration date—this day was to be my last day on earth. As I previously experienced in my life, I continue to be given extensions. I believe we receive extensions of time to figure out life to complete our mission. Since birth, my dash has continued to lengthen. After all, our dash is what we live.

Even though it's been over two years since that terrifying day, it feels more like a story I read many years ago. Sometimes when recalling this event, it feels more like a nightmare, even though it had a miraculous outcome. I sometimes forget about this event or believe none of this ever happened. My "expiration date" along with the many months that followed were filled with much drama and trauma. This experience constantly swirls through my head, causing me to recall those months. At times, I find myself conflicted with rumination and worry.

This constant rumination causes fear and bouts of overwhelming self-doubt. If not careful, I find this leads to doom and gloom thinking. I often felt like my head was going to explode, so I had to find a way to put all of it behind me. I continue to overlay those rough and painful memories with perky positive thoughts to bury the old. I use a psychological technique, thought blocking, to move past these old dreadful thoughts.

It all started the week prior to my "expiration date"; I experienced shortness of breath. I was able to muster the courage to schedule an appointment to see my primary care doctor. I wasn't fully convinced it was only allergies or asthma. I knew deep down something more was wrong. When I arrived at my appointment, to prove "nothing is wrong with me," I ran up two flights of stairs with no problem. Ah-ha, the only noticeable problem—a mild shortness of breath, and again I rationalized this by telling myself, *I'm sixty-eight and a little out of shape; nothing unusual about that, that's normal.* After I checked in, the nurse took me into an exam room, instructed me to remove my upper garments, and lie down on the table.

The nurse took my blood pressure and pulse and listened to my breathing. Within minutes, another nurse wheeled in an EKG machine and began sticking the sensor pads onto my chest. Within a few minutes, the reading was complete. She removed the pads, tore the paper from the printer, and left the room. She told me not to move or get up. Within seconds, the doctor returned to tell me they were calling an ambulance to transport me to the emergency room. Then he quickly left the room.

Holy crap, an ambulance taking me to the emergency room. No freaking way this is happening to me. I've got to get out of here.

I remembered while driving to my appointment, a still, soft voice repeatedly whispered in my ear, "You are out of time, get to the hospital." That same voice and message continued throughout my doctor's visit, but now it was more incessant. That voice echoing in my head created an urgency that I didn't have time to wait for an ambulance. Convinced I was out of time, I quickly put on my shirt, jumped off the table, and opened the door to find the coast clear. I ran out of the room and down the stairs. I jumped into my van and headed to Saint Luke's East Hospital. *Warning! Do Not Attempt to Drive Yourself to the Hospital in the Case of Emergency! This move was insane on My Part!*

While driving to the hospital and fighting to remain conscious, many thoughts ran through my mind. My first thought: *I need to call Gloria to let her know what's happening and if she would please call my daughters and son.*

By now, that still, soft voice was rapidly repeating the message. When I arrived at the hospital, I found an open parking spot directly in front of the emergency room entrance. *Is this a blessing or just luck?* As soon as I walked through the front door, I became very lightheaded and started to black out. An observant nurse grabbed my arm and helped me make it to the examination room.

Gloria and I had been seeing each other for about two years, and she reflected on this moment in time. "I remember it being about one thirty in the afternoon when I received the most frightening phone call from Jim. He was explaining he had been to see the doctor and they wanted to send him by ambulance to the hospital because his heart rate was well over 150. But Jim wasn't in an ambulance. He was driving himself to the hospital. *Why is he driving himself? Why couldn't he wait a minute?* I would take him. But Jim doesn't wait for anybody. He couldn't even wait for the ambulance. I certainly didn't realize the urgency of the situation, or the panic Jim was in. He asked me to call his daughters to let them know their dad was on his way to Saint Luke's East. That should have been a big red flag as to how serious things were. But Jim always did a fabulous job of hiding anything that might be wrong…minimizing the situation. So I don't think I was that alarmed…not just yet."

After having another EKG, I was quickly moved onto a gurney, where I lost consciousness.

Upon regaining consciousness, I found I had landed myself in a hospital room. Disoriented, I had no memory of where or how or what had transpired to cause me to be there. *What time is it? What day is it?* I was confused, weak, and exhausted. For some reason, I kept dozing in and out of sleep. Then the doctor came by my room to explain what had happened and to bring me up to date. He explained when I arrived at the hospital, I lost consciousness in the emergency room. They performed an EKG (electrocardiography) that indicated a heart rate of 150 beats a minute. The doctor referred to this as atrial fibrillation. Soon after, I went into heart failure. The coronary angiogram showed a major blockage in my heart. I was at an infarct rate of 75 percent (20 percent of my heart was functional). The medical team determined I would need four stents in my heart and it had to be shocked back into rhythm.

In sixty-eight years, I never had any symptoms of heart problems, was never hospitalized for any heart issue or any other organ issues. I was only hospitalized for three knee surgeries, a broken wrist, and a broken elbow. Shocking, but the reality is, if this can happen to me even with my medical history, it can happen to *you*!

The doctor informed me of the plan for recovery. The doctors were banking on my blood pressure increasing, with the help of a new medication, and that, in turn, would increase my heart function. The doctor believed the increased blood flow would allow the stents to kick in to restore some percentage of my heart function. They told me to anticipate staying in the hospital for another twenty-four to forty-eight hours so they could regulate and monitor my medications. Then when I stabilized, I could go home. It amazed me I would go home so soon, especially considering my weakness and inability to keep my balance to even walk.

I guess they hoped for a miracle if and when the medications kicked in. So did I.

On day three, I went home with thirteen different medications and a walker. After all those procedures and medications and still with low blood pressure, I was going home to an empty house. I was afraid, so sick, and weak. I could not walk even with the assistance of the walker.

Reentry was very awkward. I couldn't get comfortable and had lost my appetite. I felt my strength waning by the hour. So much so, I could barely stand even with the support of the walker.

In my current state, being home alone, my world suddenly became smaller, and I grew worrisome I wasn't going to recover. This is when faith and fear started a continuous and relentless tug of war. I became more frightened and uncertain, filled with anxiety that was through the roof, more than any other time in my life. I doubted every inch of my being, anything I had ever done in life. My emotions took over, and I questioned if I ever really had any faith at all. Then came the would-haves, should-haves, and could-haves, all the way back in time when I gave a guy a dirty look while in the checkout line at Walmart to stealing an ink pen from work to lying on an application for a job. The continuous flood of emotions, thoughts, and over-the-top anxiety was more than I had ever experienced and more than I ever thought I could handle.

That first night, my fear kept me from sleep. My mind filled with thoughts and worry; I tossed and turned the entire night. In hyper mode, I used the urinal every few minutes.

Finally, morning arrived. I couldn't take the worry and fear anymore. I could feel myself getting weaker by the minute. I almost passed out. Honestly, I knew this was it, I was dying.

Moribund explains that with these types of "near-death experiences," our minds can take us to some very dark places. In times like this, another person is needed to become a sounding board to help you return to earth.

Convinced this would be my last night, I went to bed, closed my eyes to relax and hoped to be able to fall into a deep sleep, which would allow me to gently cross over. I waited and waited and waited, but nothing happened. Considering what I had been through, I can now admit I was testing the waters to see if it was really my time to go. It apparently wasn't my time to leave the mother ship. After a period of lying in bed with exhaustive racing thoughts, I sat up and painfully and slowly made my way to the living room to the recliner. This was my favorite chair. This chair was made for me. I had logged many deep sleeps in that chair, or what I term as "pre-sleep".

The primary disadvantage of living alone is you are living alone. Not having a companion, a partner, an overseer, another set of eyes and ears is not much fun and lacks fulfillment. Human beings are not created to live life alone. Humans were built for cohabitation, to be monogamous, even some will suggest polygamy was likely present in the human past (Cacioppo, Fowler, and Christakis 2009). It is significant in one's life to know someone who truly knows you inside and out and is in the trenches with you. That person who can always tell you the truth and is always free to give their opinion that someone who you can trust and respect unconditionally. To add to that, it is special to have a partner who innately listens to your breathing patterns, knows when you are having a nightmare, and wakes you up when they hear a noise like someone is in the house, thus creating a significant connection and bond in the relationship. I truly desire this, again. One last time.

So being alone was enough to send my anxiety through the roof. I knew for certain I needed to go to the hospital for low blood pressure and my anxiety. I felt certain I was going to pass out and wondered what would happen if I did and who would find me and when? I thought for a moment and decided not to call an ambulance, cognizant of the cost and how long before they would arrive (maybe too late). The out-of-pocket expense would be around two thousand dollars.

So, I called a friend to see if he was available to drive me to Saint Luke's East emergency room. He came quickly and I made it into his car. As we were leaving my driveway, he asked me, "Did you say you wanted me to take you to Saint Luke's?" I answered, "That's correct." Before I completed the sentence he said, "I'm not going to drive all the way to Lee's Summit when we have a hospital here in Independence." I said, "If you can't, I understand. Now stop the car so I can get out and start walking." I continued, "Even if it kills me trying, I'm going to Saint Luke's East where my doctors are." He said, "Wow, if you're that determined, I will take you."

When we arrived, I walked into the emergency room and again lost consciousness. I was in heart failure again, but this time I woke up in an ambulance on life support, headed to Saint Luke's Hospital on the Plaza. I could hear voices in the background at the emergency room and now in the ambulance. I heard them say something about heart failure again and they were having difficulty getting me restarted. I was being transferred to Saint Luke's on the Plaza so I would receive the level of care I needed for my present condition. Now the decision would be made if the attempt to repair my heart showed any signs of improvement and increased my longevity. The attempt to rejuvenate my existing heart might be futile. With that in mind, would transplantation be an option to consider. It might be my only chance of survival, the only way out alive—this is where it becomes very interesting and conspicuously intense.

What I came to realize is optimism is sustainable when you can find something to be grateful for in your life and something you can count on. My entire existence now hung by a thread, and my life would be forever changed. I was convinced I would never again reach a level of existence or happiness equivalent to my prior life. Could I adjust to this new situation so suddenly without some resistance or pushback? It dawned on me that happiness is temporary and situational, but finding purpose gives deeper meaning to life. So daily, I am on a quest to find purposeful meaning in my life and others.

> **_Lesson in Resilience:_** Finding purpose or finding success? Success, a global term, is often overused and misused. The word has specific meaning that can only be defined by each orator used. Success is a term used to express completion at a higher level of performance, career accomplishment, and/or financial gain and prosperity. Success is not usually a word associated in terms of medical recovery. When I initially started my recovery journey, I set a goal of returning to the same level of emotional and physical quality I had prior to June 28, 2021. Along the way, I have redefined and adjusted my definition of success. Am I considered a failure if I only achieve 80 percent of my goal? Sometimes, reality is harsh and adjusting outcomes is essential. It doesn't mean you're settling if you've done everything humanly possible. It just means your new reality at the time is your success. Embrace and keep moving forward, gain resilience.

CHAPTER 7

Throw in the Towel or Wait

A man's heart plans his way, but the Lord determines his steps.
— PROVERBS 16:9 (ESV)

I'm awake, but where am I? I must be in the middle of a bad dream—dazed and delusional, but I am conscious enough to ask out loud: "What is happening to me?" A voice replied, "You are being transferred from Saint Luke's East to Saint Luke's on the Plaza. Your heart stopped a second time and again you experienced heart failure." Hearing those words drained me of life. I knew with 100 percent certainty I would peacefully cross over to eternity as life escaped my body. I thought, *Don't leave, it's not time, I'm not done, I have so much more to accomplish.* It was as if I was summoning my soul back. I knew my end was near. I had run out of cat lives. I could tell my body and organs were shutting down and telling me, "It's time to go. We are beat up and damaged beyond repair, time to throw in the towel." Then I felt the vehicle stop. We must have arrived at the hospital.

Once inside and within seconds, they admitted me and wheeled me into a room and took vitals. Next, they wheeled me to the operating room. I was informed they were going to install a central venous port so they could draw blood more easily and introduce medications quickly and painlessly.

Following the procedure, I returned to my room to find a nurse waiting to place an IV in my arm. Then the phlebotomist came to draw seven vials of blood. With so much blood drawn over the last week or so, I grew worrisome. My thoughts began running wild, taking me down the rabbit hole again. After all, they drew seven vials of blood all at once. I knew drawing this amount of blood would cause me to become hypovolemic, a condition in which the liquid portion of blood is too low.

I needed more information, so I did a little internet research regarding how much blood can safely be drawn from our bodies.

My research showed the body can easily handle the removal of eighty-eight vials of blood drawn daily and over 500 vials drawn weekly without feeling any adverse effects, and I worried about seven vials (National Heart, Lung, and Blood Institute 2022).

The capacity of the human body is incomprehensible.

The process of maintaining homeostasis of the physiological processes is an amazing feat of the human body. I learned while researching that red blood cells carry oxygen and the protein hemoglobin, which carries oxygen throughout the body and removes carbon dioxide from tissues. White cells fight infection and are part of your immune system. They end bleeding by sealing cuts on blood vessel walls. The right preparation for your blood draw depends on what is being tested (American Society of Hematology n.d.).

My daughters informed me that since I'd been admitted, the doctors had focused entirely on the revitalization of my heart. The doctors had attempted to increase my blood pressure through the use of medication, hoping these would normalize my heart function. Unfortunately, for the last thirty days, the attempt had been pushing blood out through my liver. They found my blood volume was low (hypovolemia), so I needed two pints of blood. The tests continued at a steady rate. They were keeping me busy. Next were an MRI, a CT scan, an EKG and so on and so on. The hospital was very thorough.

When I'm in the presence of one of these doctors, I sense confidence and assertiveness. I am at peace, reassured I'm in good hands. No grass has any chance of growing under anyone's feet at this hospital.

Due to my level of anxiety, fear, bouts of incoherence, and medical condition, I decided to give two of my daughters, Taia and Ashley, medical power of attorney. Both are registered nurses, and both worked for many years in cardiovascular units. Is all this happenstance or Divine plan?

The medication failed to keep my heart pumping. Therefore, the doctors decided to install the world's smallest heart pump, the Impella® pump, which is inserted through an opening in the groin. Once this catheterization passes the aortic valve through the femoral artery, it provides support to the right side of the heart for up to fourteen days.

The hospital staff called my family to the hospital. Upon their arrival, they and the doctors gathered around my bed. The doctors informed us that the pump, along with the medicine, could keep me alive for approximately fourteen more days, but they would place me on the heart transplant list immediately. And due to the severity of my heart condition, I would be placed at the highest priority tier. Having A-positive blood also provided me the highest probability of receiving a new heart before time ran out. The downside of installation of the pump required me to lie flat on my back. The head of the bed could be raised only 30 degrees when I needed to eat or drink. Being flat on my back and not being allowed to get out of bed meant using a bedpan only—ugh!

Around August 3, 2021, the doctors decided to relocate the balloon pump from my groin up to the subclavian artery in my chest. I had already been in bed thirty days, so to keep me from losing more muscle mass, the doctors wanted me to increase my mobility. According to the National Council on Aging, for every day you lie in bed, you lose four days out of bed (2021). Oh, no!

On the morning of August 5, the doctors and nurses came into my room and gathered around my bed. They began, "We have something we need to tell you." Wow, what now? My heart nearly stopped. Then I heard, "We found you a new heart." I wanted to jump out of bed and do a happy dance.

While in the hospital, I read a poem a friend sent me. It touches on the theme of rescue. I paraphrase this theme as "clear the brush away" in your mind and your life. Bottom line—only small things matter; everything is a small thing. Please understand I have always lived my life like a "superhero," always trying to save the world and everybody in it—now I focus on saving my own.

> **_Lesson in Resilience:_** While growing up, mother often said to me, "Patience is a virtue, a virtue you will never have." I hope mother got the word that during my heart journey, I gained and experienced much patience. Waiting, without impatience or anger, develops resilience.

CHAPTER 8

Fear of the Unknown

Too many of us are not living our dreams because we are living our fears.

— ATTRIBUTED TO LES BROWN

The psychological term for fear of the unknown is xenophobia (Stanborough 2020). Many sources define fear of the unknown as the tendency to be afraid of something you have no information about on any level. Some people report that when facing the unknown, they become physically sick to their stomach with increased anxiety. Others report symptoms of rapid, shallow breathing, increased heart rate, tensing of muscles, weakness, and glucose spikes. If the fear is short-lived, there is no problem, but when the fear is constant, it may have effects on one's long-term health. My mother was a worrier, which led to constant anxiety, which in turn led to catastrophizing or cognitive distortions (Aucoin and Bhardwaj 2016).

It is important to accept that fear is healthy and natural but also is anger. Feeling fear is having the capacity to be afraid and is part of normal brain functioning. In fact, lack of fear might be a sign of other problems. Anxiety or fear arises when a person is caught off guard or lacks information and facts of the impending doom, or fear of the unknown. All of us have a strong need to be in control of any given situation. It's natural, and if we get into a situation we can't control, then our anxiety will increase.

Most things in our life we can't control, but the three things we should learn to control are: our thoughts, our feelings, and our actions (behaviors). There are many factors we don't and can't control; however, focus on the choices available to you and make it the best choice for the best outcome. Always assess the situation you're in at the moment. Look at all the variables and determine what you can control and what factors are beyond your control. This method seems to help lower anxiety and stress and gives us some sense of control. If psychological symptoms or previous history of mental disorders exist, this will greatly increase the propensity for fear and increased anxiety.

Living in today's world, especially over the last four years, adjusting and coping with COVID, I believe we are more stress-prone and living in fear than ever before. Merely letting go of repressed emotions makes us vulnerable, which in turn makes us more fearful, which only feeds existing neurosis and psychosis. It is important to know that the more anxiety injected into a person's world, the more that person will revert to old behaviors and feelings. So, no matter what new behaviors or thoughts are learned, anxiety will sometimes cause us to peel back the newly learned for the old to be revealed again. The level of our fear is determined by the existing fear we already possess and reveals the stimulus that causes triggers. The more we harbor fear on the inside, the more our perception of the world becomes a terrifying and guarded existence. Whatever is repressed in us will become our skewed perception of life and the world.

Fear is an uncomfortable experience accompanied by a wide range of emotions. I remember experiencing my first fear symptoms of illness prior to June 28, 2021, that hurled me into a fear and worry mode. It impacted most of my thoughts, feelings, and behaviors in my life. It especially impacted my ability to make decisions and to sleep, but primarily, it impacted my outlook on what would, could, and should happen. This led me to constantly build various scenarios that only added more fear and worry to an already compounding unknown. The more I experienced the unknown fear, the more worry became constant worry that would eventually turn into chronic stress.

This engulfed everything in my life, implications for survival. I found myself getting scared by just imagining the what-ifs. With or without medical issues, life can be terrifying, especially when back-to-back to back tragic events occur. The cycle of life allows that all the people we know and love will eventually suffer and die. The process of life is biological, the purpose of life is spiritual. During my journey, I listened to my wounded heart (literally) and tried feeling all the love from all the people I know and love. I tried to recall all those precious times with each and every person I had ever encountered. I only want to see, hear, think, and do only the positive.

After a while, I began to see the break in the clouds to see many, many loving moments. After a while, I could feel the shift when I became grounded in love and faith. Many of us have faith if life is moving along in a positive direction. I see faith as a deeper spiritual understanding that surpasses religion, that allows your loving heart to show through. It is important to remember the heart doesn't have room to possess both hatred and love. You choose, but you can't have both. The conversion of the heart is to transition from judgmental to embracing appreciation. Every day is a new opportunity to change your life.

I always fall back on His promise that if I trust I will find new strength and I will soar high on wings like eagles. He promises I will run and not grow weary and faint. Remember: the fears you don't face become your limits. Read that again.

Lesson in Resilience: I have failed many times during my life. I have always taken the difficult goals and challenges, always confronted my fears and shortcomings. This is when I gained the most resilience.

CHAPTER 9

Are You Prepared to Leave Well?

—

"When a man sees his end, he wants to know there was some purpose to his life."

—MARCUS AURELIUS, GLADIATOR

Has the focus of your life thus far been living your dash or on your end date? Which is the most beneficial use of your time? Which will be more relaxing and create more memories? Before answering these questions, ask yourself this: If your end-of-life affairs are in order and you are prepared to leave this world, will you answer differently?

This subject matter is something everyone avoids. Before reading any further, please take a moment and close your eyes. Take a deep breath through your nose and hold that breath for about thirty seconds while focused on your heart rate, then slowly exhale through your mouth. Then say to yourself silently, "It is okay to read the words in this chapter. By doing so, it will not cause my death but will allow me to be prepared for the end, for when I take my last breath and leave my family free of most burdens.

Now you are better prepared to read and accept the contents of this chapter. Good reading.

Most of us, if not all, never seem ready for the end of life. The folks whom I've seen in hospice, I have witnessed their resistance crossing over into the other side, to eternity. Then there are those folks who cross over gently and quietly, wearing a peaceful smile. These folks are certain where they are going and are prepared to leave well.

My grandfather was in the funeral business, and he often remarked that everyone avoids the topic of death even though it is known that no one gets out alive. The one topic everybody absolutely avoids is the subject of death. I have heard folks say and believe it to be true, "If I talk about it then it will happen." Really, if you are that powerful with words, then will yourself to live forever and while you are at it, include us all. So far, I haven't heard of anyone being successful with this method. The most important takeaway from this chapter is this—before that extended illness or that final breath, leave your family well. Try to fast forward your life to the end and think of the worst-case scenario. Then visualize family and loved ones in the midst of grieving your death. Think beyond yourself for a moment—is this a good time to place heavy burdens and decisions on those left behind?

The most needed and toughest question each of us should be answering now and not later is: Are my affairs in order so upon my death, my family is not left with the burden of making decisions on responsibilities I could have easily taken care of ahead of time? While amid my most difficult time during pretransplant, alone with medical complications and at my lowest level of coherency, I was forced to make these heavy decisions. I fortunately have two daughters, Taia and Ashley, who are equipped to handle this level of responsibility to have power over my medical care and financial affairs. Even at a low level of coherency, it was an easy decision since they are both registered nurses and both worked for many years in cardiac units.

I was not prepared for this blindsiding, out-of-left-field life-altering emergency. I would have never guessed this could happen to me. My not being prepared and putting last-minute burdens on them and their families caused additional time and stress they didn't need or expect, and what a huge embarrassment to me. It is important to have a living will and medical and financial power of attorney drawn up before this type of emergency or any life-altering emergency happens. Please consult with a family law attorney and make sure your DNR is signed and notarized. Also, make a list of all passwords, checking and savings account numbers and passwords, monthly bill accounts and amounts. This is something I advise everyone to have in place well before life gets to a critical stage.

Keep these documents in a fireproof vault or with your attorney. Please be prepared for the unexpected and when and if you are blindsided by the unknown. You can plan your life for "all the knowns" but it is impossible to plan for "all the unknowns." That is why we call them emergencies or accidents. We didn't expect and didn't anticipate these occurrences. This preparation process is commonly referred to as Advance Care Planning, ACP, and helps maintain your dignity and values if you find yourself in the middle of being forced to make medical treatment decisions. It also gives you the certainty and protection by appointing a trustworthy, confident person to watch your back.

LET'S BREAK THE PROCESS INTO FOUR STAGES:

First Stage: Think about what you would want if you had to make difficult choices for medical care or end of life.

- Who to contact in an emergency? Make a list of family, friends, neighbors, and spiritual advisors.
- Make a list of medical teams
- Make a list of prescriptions and medical history (especially when traveling/overseas).
- Make a list of things you would like taken care of and a list of people you don't want contacted and people not to see.

Second Stage: Choose a spokesperson to speak for you or appoint someone and give them power of attorney.

- Lives close or could travel to be at my side if need be.
- Able to talk about sensitive topics and respect my wishes.
- Are reliable and responsible.
- Can take varying opinions of medical personnel and family to make rational decisions.
- Can be fair and flexible with decisions.

Third Stage: Plan a time when loved ones can be present to hear your views on end of life and health care providers.

- Pick a person who can handle big-time responsibility without any self-doubts. Be sure they match your

values, preferences, and wishes, even if they're somewhat different.
- Let family know if you filled out a durable power of attorney for healthcare document to appoint your spokesperson.
- Be sure to cover your beliefs, life-sustaining treatments, your mental health preferences, list of names for the medical team to contact and not contact, what you value, and what you want to happen after your death.

Fourth Stage: a personal recording (audio, video, letter) to share your wishes.

- Even if you have completed documents left with your attorney, family members can still have reassurance and lasting memories of your desires and making correct decisions on your behalf. This will give family and healthcare professional reassurance they are doing the right thing (Planning My Way n.d.).

After reading this chapter, do your initial answers to the opening questions change? Now maybe you have more things to consider. I hope.

Interesting side note: I've read several studies that report positive outcomes for families who are prepared for end-of-life care and final arrangements report improved bereavement outcomes. Out of 143 participants, 57 percent of participants were very practically prepared for death, while only 29 percent were emotionally prepared. Three qualitative themes related to practical and emotional preparation were identified: Ambiguity and uncertainty; kind of support from the system; how death is perceived by the family and support system. More research is needed on how to emotionally prepare for a relative's death (Motla 2023).

In her book, The Top Five Regrets of the Dying: A Life Transformed by the Dearly Departing, Bronnie Ware lists:

1. I wish I'd had the courage to live a life true to myself, not the life others expected of me.
2. I wish I hadn't worked so hard.
3. I wish I had the courage to express my feelings.
4. I wish I had stayed in touch with my (extended family) friends.
5. I wish I had let myself be happier (2009).

Sonia Sonia, Director, Career Counselor, Personal Marketing, Career Coaching, Vocational Advising, Guidance, Job Path Counseling, on her LinkedIn page, states the following:

- Be true to yourself; live a life that aligns with your own values, dreams, and desires, rather than trying to meet the expectations of others. Follow your own path, embrace your authenticity.
- Prioritize what truly matters; don't get caught up in the pursuit of material possessions or societal notions of success. Instead, focus on the things and relationships that bring you joy, love, and fulfillment.
- Express your feelings; don't suppress your emotions or keep your thoughts and feelings hidden. Practice honest and open communication, expressing your emotions and needs in a respectful manner. This can lead to deeper connections and more meaningful relationships

- Cultivate and maintain friendships; make time for your friends and nurture those relationships. Prioritize human connections and invest in meaningful connections that bring support, joy, and shared experiences.
- Choose happiness; allow yourself to experience joy and happiness. Don't postpone happiness for the future or wait for external circumstances to dictate your well-being. Find joy in the present moment and actively seek out activities and experiences that bring you happiness (LinkedIn 2023).

Lesson in Resilience: The toughest reality to accept is that nobody gets out alive—each one of us has an end date. Acceptance and a deep understanding of death and dying will free you of the burden of fear of the unknown and constant worry. Age comes to us all and if blessed, we grow old. Die with memories, not dreams.

CHAPTER 10

Heart Transplantation

___

When I woke on August 5, 2021, I drank a protein shake for breakfast and tried, unsuccessfully, to get out of bed to use the restroom. I knew the clock was ticking and I was at the end of my time on earth. I prayed I would hear today they had found me a new ticker. I knew I was losing mobility, and I was too weak to use a walker. Four nurses had to pick me up and put me in a wheelchair. Then I was wheeled into the restroom.

About the time they returned me to bed, a doctor came in to tell me some lifesaving news. They found a match for a donor heart, and if everything checked out as expected, a doctor would be here with the heart around four p.m. today. Then around five p.m., I would be taken down to the operating room to be prepped for surgery. I could not believe what I just heard. I couldn't hold back all my emotions, so I went ahead and burst into tears with overwhelming jubilation. If I could have, I would have jumped out of bed, breaking into the happy dance.

When I got the news of my new heart's arrival, it seemed as though time had stopped. I remember staring at the clock on the wall and swore the hands had frozen in place. Minutes felt like hours. Finally, five o'clock rolled around, and transportation came to my room to take me to prep for surgery. After prep, they placed me in another room, and my entire family came in one by one to give me love and offer encouragement, hugs, and embrace. During this time, I noticed something very peculiar; I was free of worry and fear. I had an all-consuming peace rushing throughout my entire being. The peace of trusting in God's promise. His promise that He will always be with me; ask and you shall receive; and if it is His will, it will be done. Knowing these three absolute truths and knowing the process and having total trust in the doctors and staff, I went into surgery totally at peace and serene ready to accept my destiny. His will.

I entered surgery on Thursday, August 5, 2021, around seven p.m. The surgery concluded around midnight. Following the completion of my heart transplant, the surgeon came out to talk to my daughters and Gloria. He advised them that the new heart was in and functioning, but he had to leave my chest cavity open until the morning when he would decide to remove a sack found next to my heart. I would be kept fully sedated until they made that decision the next morning.

As planned, around eleven a.m., they took me back into surgery and removed the sack. I was moved to the CVICU (Cardiovascular Intensive Care Unit), where I remained on a ventilator until I could breathe on my own. I remained on that ventilator until the morning of August 7, Saturday. That morning, they placed me in a chair with a safety belt to keep me from falling out of the chair. I was unconscious and delirious and had no memories of anything until Sunday afternoon. I didn't wake up until my daughters returned to visit. I remember when they arrived; they looked at me weirdly, saying, "He's not in his right mind. He's delirious; he's not making any sense. He doesn't know what he's saying." But to me it all made perfect sense. I looked at them and thought, *They aren't listening to what I'm saying. They're messing with me. Why are they messing with me after all I've been through, duh?*

The more coherent I became, the more I noticed the number of monitors, bags of medication, and fluids plugged into my body. I saw all the bright lights, heard the noise from machines, nurses checking equipment and checking my vitals, blood pressure, blood sugar, breathing, and heart monitor. In the days following the heart surgery, I was being pushed to the edge of difficulty, so I had to push it all on Him completely. I know to fully trust Him because if I fall, He will catch me or He will teach me to fly, if it is His plan. I became hypersensitive to sound and unable to sleep, but soon a peacefulness came over me and I was asleep in a moment and slept like a baby. I continued in the CVICU, for seven to eight days, then I was moved to a special care unit. The nurse brought me a heart-shaped pillow, which was awesome. I keep this pillow next to me to this day as a reminder of gratitude and blessings.

Starting August 17, a physical therapist came to my room for one hour daily. Physical therapy was most challenging since I wasn't allowed to use my arms to push or pull until my sternum was completely healed. After transplantation, you are expected to wear a "heart hugger," which protects the integrity of the sternal closure after surgery. I was given an absolute to not use my arms and hands when getting up or sitting down to avoid injury to the sternum. This required a lot of focus. I was able to gain some mobility, to a point. I continued to progress up to walking forty feet.

For many months following my transplantation, I've been asked a particular question frequently, "Now that you have a new heart, do you feel differently, or are you a different person? Do you feel weird or something, like you're possessed?" Well, my consistent reply has been, "Of course not; it's an organ, it doesn't feel anything, I'm the same person but now with a healthy heart." Fast forward to current day and knowing about these comments in the forefront of my mind this entire time, I have noted many comments from others like, "You have changed; you're a different person."

Thus, it dawned on me after many hours of thinking and reflecting on these ideas that the heart is much more than just an organ that performs functions beyond simply pumping blood throughout our bodies. After all, I now own a healthy heart that was donated from a different body and has the tissue and DNA of that donor. I am aware that the vagal nerves, a group of nerves found in the heart, control memory and adaptation. In addition, the heart is a synchronizing force that transmits both personality traits and emotional data.

About 3 to 5 percent of transplant recipients have reported personality changes, preferences and dislikes, and temperamental differences with their donors. After receiving a transplant, one recipient reported developing a need for beer and fried chicken. Given that she was a vegetarian and abstained from alcohol, that was very strange. Upon analyzing the diverse belief systems, most of them concur that memories are exclusively retained within the brain.

Many have faced criticism or ridicule for sharing strange anecdotes, which could stifle interest and prevent more people from coming forward to support different claims (Inspector, Kutz, and David 2004).

Scientists made a breakthrough in 1991. It was found that each human heart contains forty to forty-five thousand specialized cells that work together to form a neural network that produces brain-like cells within the heart. This region of the heart is known as the "little brain" and is made up of these forty thousand specialized cells, which are also known as censoring dendrites. Researchers have found these cells are capable of independent thought, the creation of a running program, memory retention independent of the cranium brain, and memory of past experiences, including the present one. This is a positive experience; therefore it's not a problem that I'm recognizing it in various areas in both my cranium (little brain in my heart) and mental mind (upper brain) (Alshami 2019).

Some people believe and are curious about if the transplant heart carries the personality of the donor, a question I am often asked. The heart is not only a pump but a center of feeling, memory, and personality. The heart, like the nervous system, possesses the properties of memory and adaptation. The heart acts as a synchronizing force within the body, a key carrier of emotional information as well as other personality keys. There are reports from heart transplant patients who experience some personality changes and the temperament of their donor.

Normally the vagus nerve innervates the heart; however, during an orthotopic heart transplant procedure, the heart becomes denervated and vagal input is impaired. This alters both the resting heart rate as well as the heart rate responses during activity and in response to exercise. Sympathetic nerve fibers release norepinephrine. My question is if my new heart's vagus nerve has been completely severed, there is no way my new heart can receive any signals from my brain. So how does it know to beat, or to function; it is a three-pound mass of tissue and muscle, how does it know. Better yet, how does the perimeter (exterior) of the heart that is made up of so many blood vessels find a source of blood to keep it alive and vibrant (Awad et al. 2016).

While cardiac denervation (loss of nerve supply) happens right away following a heart transplant, cardiac reinnervation (complete loss of afferent and efferent nerve connections) is a varied phenomenon that is currently up for debate in the field of heart transplantation. Nonetheless, a wealth of research has been done to support the theory of cardiac reinnervation, which has been demonstrated to happen in 40 to 70 percent of patients sometime after heart transplantation. It is also possible for sensory reinnervation to happen after cardiac transplantation. In order for sympathetic reinnervation to occur, nerve terminals outside the heart that are attached to nerve terminals in the transplanted heart must function. Reestablished connections between pre- and postsynaptic adrenergic components of the synapse were linked with restored presynaptic nerve terminals in heart transplant recipients (Awad et al. 2016).

Studies using microscopy show sympathetic nerves growing along the coronary blood vessels and the anastomosis between the donor heart and the recipient portions of the myocardium.

Cardiac reinnervation after heart transplantation reduces the correlation between heart rate at rest and the predicted intrinsic heart rate, causes nerve release from the cardiac nerve terminals in response to exercise and pharmacological stimuli, allows for the return of neuronal control over HR and ventricular contractility, and improves exercise performance after heart transplantation. Sympathetic reinnervation is observed later after heart transplantation due to the slow regrowth of nerves. Those who were reinnervated had a lengthier period between receiving a heart transplant and enrolling in the research than those who were denervated. While parasympathetic reinnervation appears to occur more than one to three years after heart transplantation, sympathetic reinnervation happens at least five to six months after heart transplantation (Awad et al. 2016).

Even after going through and being able to endure the entire process—pretransplant, the transplant, and after the heart transplant recovery—I still find it incredibly difficult to comprehend the wonder and magnificence of how everything comes together to prolong life with such remarkable quality. The statistics on transplant surgical survival, which indicate an 85 to 90 percent survival rate, are interesting. Merely 15 to 20 percent of patients pass away within a year after the procedure, but after that, the percentage drops off quickly, averaging just 4 percent per year for the following eighteen years. They anticipated that 50 percent of patients would still be alive after ten years, and only 15 percent after twenty. The quality of the donor heart, the donor's age, the necessity for inotropic assistance in the past, and the length of graft ischemia are only a few of the variables that affect longevity (Ransford et al. 2000). However, as I progress, I am realizing that maintaining one's quality of life and recuperating never truly ends—until one's final breath. I am appreciative of each and every breath and stride forward. Thank you, donor and donor family.

A side note: I discovered profound meditation helped both before and after the transplant. I primarily practice two types of deep meditation. The first focuses on relaxation. The environment is frequently prepared for deep relaxation meditation: candles or low lighting, pleasant scents, background music that is calming and even hypnotic, etc. You can either lie down or sit while you meditate. The second is primarily concerned with conscious awareness. Typically, the person meditating is seated. Deep awareness meditation is experienced when the meditator has found a comfortable balance between vigilance and letting go. It is a natural outcome of advanced mindfulness training. Without interruption, awareness of the breath (or sound, sensations, ideas, etc.) persists; the mind may take note of additional stimuli or perceptions; there's no impulse to cling to them (Mindworks 2022).

Since we are on the subject of the heart, I think it's appropriate to inject a piece from Pastor Rick Warren I read a while ago illustrating the various types of hearts, metaphorically speaking. I thought it appropriate to include in this part of my story, giving additional insight to accepting and embracing differences in others.

A person with a harsh tongue has an angry heart
A person with a negative tongue has a fearful heart
A person with a reactive tongue has an unsettled heart

A person with a boastful tongue has an insecure heart
A person with a filthy tongue has an impure heart
A person with a judgmental tongue has a bitter heart
On the flip side:
A person who encourages has a graceful heart
A person who speaks gently has a loving heart
A person who speaks truthfully has an honest heart
- Pastor Rick Warren (2020)

A valuable lesson I learned from this experience is when at the lowest, roughest time in life, realize if it is in His plan, He will put you on a wake-up list to get your attention. He will provide if it is His plan that I was created for. I was being pushed to the edge of life so I had to rely on Him, trusting if I fell, He'd catch me, or He would teach me to fly, soaring on the wings of eagles.

So far from June 28, 2021, until now, my journey has been incredible. No matter that I lived it and no matter how many times I read and reread the words on these pages, it is unimaginable and certainly unfathomable that I'm here today. I am so blessed. Two of my biggest challenges during this journey have been the major weight of my emotional tug of war and the physical challenges, which we address in the next chapter. This period was pretty rough and rigorous and at times debilitating and included several setbacks. I equate this part of the journey as trying to climb a glass mountain. Have you tried doing that lately? Read On.

> **_Lesson in Resilience:_** The answer to getting through a heart transplant is resilience. First, diagnosis of heart failure is a substantial blow to a person's

invincibility. Second, a positive outlook is a tremendous advantage to surviving and thriving. Third, learn the difference of being vulnerable, but realizing invincible. Remember, avoid negative thinking, trust in yourself, and seize opportunities that are in your reach.

CHAPTER 11

Physical Challenges of Recovery

Following the transplant, my recovery process was far from textbook, let's say unique to my situation. Recovery was continuous and brutal, with many setbacks and comebacks. A typical recovery from a heart transplant normally takes three to six months. However, age and illnesses may prolong the recovery period (Lindberg et al. 2020). In my case, full recovery was extended to almost two years.

Since this was my first illness and hospital stay, the days to follow were difficult, not only the physical challenge but the added stress of the emotional challenges. The physical challenge became an inside game that challenged my resilience. Since I had made it this far, I was cautiously optimistic, yet eyes wide shut to what lay ahead. At this juncture, I felt drained of life, or whatever surpasses exhaustion. I was relying on faith and learned resilience to carry me to the finish line. I thought since I had a new heart, I would bounce back to my pretransplant physicality rapidly. However, this was not the case. I was concerned that my lack of energy was to become my new normal, leaving me in a constant state of exhaustion.

I questioned how I was going to complete rehab with this level of physical and emotional drain before I could return to what I knew to be normal for me. As my coherency returned, I began noticing the number of monitors, bags of medication and fluids plugged into my body. All the bright lights, noise from the machines, nurses checking equipment, checking my blood pressure, blood sugar, breathing, and the heart monitor, made my getting any quality sleep impossible. Being in a constant state of sleep deprivation, I was forced to resort to medications. Finally, I was now able to sleep like a baby if they would shut off the lights and leave me alone—well, not too alone.

I remained in CVICU for seven or eight days. This special unit only cares for transplant patients and is trained specifically for ensuring recovery. This focus on recovery is likely why the nurse on duty gave me the heart shaped pillow.

The unit's experience means they likely knew it would be an awesome gift at just the right time. I imagine I'm not the only former patient who keeps their heart pillow nearby to serve as a reminder of life, gratitude, and blessings. Around August 17, 2021, I began physical therapy (PT) in my room for an hour every day.

As I mentioned earlier, I found the most difficult part of recovery was that I wasn't allowed to use my arms to assist me in standing until my sternum was completely healed.

Therefore, physical therapy became a real challenge emotionally as well as physically following transplant. The heart hugger I had to wear continuously saved me from additional injury several times during my recovery.

One example of the effectiveness of the heart hugger occurred during my early recovery when I was too weak to sit up or move out of my bed. The nurses were adamant I get out of bed and, to prove their point, did not allow me to use a bedpan or diapers. Because of the sternal closure, I wasn't allowed to grab onto anything to pull or push my body for fear of additional injury. To assist me with getting out of bed, a machine was brought to my bedside. The nurses sat me up on the edge of the bed, placed a device around my chest with straps over my shoulders, then clicked a strap that came out from the machine, a pulley. The pulley was released to provide extra slack so there was no tension. I placed both feet on the base of the machine, and at the top of the machine were two metal arms spaced wider than my body for me to reach over to grab. Now they were ready to crank me to a standing position to be wheeled into the restroom to be lowered onto the toilet.

As the nurse started cranking the pulley to raise me up, I knew instantly the harness was not fitted properly, I knew I was not secured. I could feel myself slipping from the harness, I yelled for him to stop cranking, I was going to fall. He totally ignored me and continued to crank to lift me. Again, I said, "Stop."

He said, "How much training have you had on this equipment? I know what I'm doing." Seriously? I continued to shout, "Stop, stop, stop." Then, I slipped out, falling to the floor, my chest throbbing. I was mad as hell.

The first words out of his mouth were, "That harness must be faulty." He said, "I've done this hundreds of times, and this is the first time I've had a problem."

I replied, "Pal, you would be wise to trust the cries of the patient and be reassuring. The patient always should be safe and secure."

At this point, he began backtracking with rapid CYAs (Cover Your Asses).

Another save for the heart hugger. Listen up, anyone: please pay attention when receiving medical care. You have the right to ask questions and/or refuse a procedure. Please don't sit back and say nothing or do nothing—be proactive—you have the right.

During my first sixteen weeks following the transplant, I had to wear the heart hugger the entire period. I had to fully focus to not use my arms and hands to pull or push, and yes, that was exhausting. One doesn't realize how much you use the arms and legs to maneuver throughout your day. This situation forced me to realize just how much I have taken for granted my appendages—this has become fully automatic not requiring any thought on my part. Both nurses and physical therapy repeatedly told me, "You don't want to disturb or tear the sternal closure because that would require your chest to be cracked open again to repair, which would be extremely painful." I might add with emphasis on extremely painful.

About fourteen days posttransplant and after starting PT, I gained enough mobility to get out of bed and walk twenty feet. In another five days, I progressed to forty feet. Once I could walk that distance, I asked if I could be moved to rehab to continue my physical therapy. However, the hospital wanted to see improved blood test results before allowing me to move to the rehab facility. Also, the facility had no beds available, so I waited another week.

A bed, finally, came available on August 16, and I was transported to a rehabilitation facility. I remained cautiously optimistic even while feeling encouraged.

During my twenty-one days in the rehabilitation center, I made some progress. However, going home alone and taking care of myself was out of the question. I knew I would require constant assistance, at least for a while.

All the trauma my body had endured and serious issues on balancing my blood results added to my recovery challenges. I was scheduled to graduate from rehab on September 8, 2021, and to go home. On September 6, the social worker came to my room to inform me that in less than two hours transport would be here to take me to a skilled nursing facility to finish my rehabilitation. My insurance had run out, and I refused to pay $800/day until released. I was in shock. A two-hour warning, really? Within two hours, transportation was at my room, ready to take me to the other facility.

For the entire two-hour wait, I begged and pleaded to be able to finish my rehab at Saint Luke's. I had such an uneasiness about leaving Saint Luke's. Remember, I had only two days to complete rehab and then go home, or so I thought. While waiting those two hours, my gut told me this transfer was not going to turn out well. Little did I know the true depth of my emotional insight. It's called *emotional intelligence*. When and if you experience this type of visceral emotion, listen and heed the warning.

The transition to the skilled nursing facility wasn't anything close to what I had imagined. I had been spoiled at Saint Luke's. Upon arrival, they placed me in quarantine. Since I left Saint Luke's so abruptly, there wasn't time to administer a rapid COVID-19 test, and the skilled facility was out of them. After settling in at the new place and looking around, I found the room to be a little on the archaic side of inpatient care. Since leaving Saint Luke's rehabilitation early, I was still on bed restrictions until physical therapy could perform my evaluation. When I saw the distance to the bathroom from my bed, between twenty to twenty-five feet with no riser on the toilet, I realized I would not be able to make it there on my own. My leg muscles were still too weak, and I didn't have the strength to rise from a sitting position to standing on my own. If I tried to get out of bed, the bed alarm would sound, and they would be in my room immediately. I was at the mercy of others for assistance. Naturally, they were short staffed. The wait time between ringing for assistance to staff arrival was around twelve minutes or longer. Thank you, COVID-19.

As predicted, in the morning physical therapy was at my bedside early to do their assessment, which took about an hour to complete. Later that same morning, occupational therapy came to complete their assessment. Both physical and occupational therapy left the schedule with me for the week, which would start the next day. Physical and occupational therapy moved along at a very fast pace. What I especially liked about the physical therapist assigned to me was her focus on the core muscle groups. The techniques she used for motivation along with a gentle nudge were laced with firmness. Following the completion of my first week, my progress was incremental. The physical therapist projected my release date as September 28, 2021. Twenty-one days after my arrival, and if I continued to progress, I should be leaving on the twenty-eighth. Now, I was pumped. I had a going home date. My laser-focus kicked in and there was no stopping me. The first week of therapy went fine with incremental progress.

On Sunday night, I ate shrimp scampi for dinner. After dinner, I was watching television when suddenly I felt my stomach churning. I said to myself, "This didn't settle quite right." I remember thinking, *Oh now what*? Around ten p.m., the nurse brought in my medicine, which I took and eventually I fell asleep. To my surprise, around two a.m. I was awakened abruptly, vomiting profusely. I looked on each side of my bed, no trash can in sight. Since I was on bed restriction, my only option was to let it go by the side of my bed onto the floor. As soon as I got a little break from the action, I hit the call button. When the nurse entered, I told her I was deathly sick, plus she could see and hear my current condition. I told her I needed an ambulance, and I needed to be transported back to Saint Luke's. I was dying. Her response, "The doctor on staff will be in around 5:30 a.m., and he will decide at that time what you need." *Are you kidding me?* After everything I have been through, I wasn't waiting for several hours for someone to decide my destiny

Plus, if I was going to die, I wanted it to be at the same place that gave me life.

So, I called 911 myself and the ambulance was there within minutes. As they wheeled me out of the facility, the nurse gave me a "how-dare-you-overrule-me" look. Boy, she looked pissed. I was quickly transported to Saint Luke's. I thought the destination was Saint Luke's East, but while en route, they received instructions to take me to Saint Luke's on the Plaza.

When we arrived in the emergency room, I only had few memories of what followed. I remember being taken to ICU before I became unconscious. I also remember asking the nurse to call Gloria. Gloria arrived at my bedside soon after I arrived in ICU, and I think I was in the middle of having a conversation with her when I stopped breathing. Gloria later told me my breathing went from deep to shallow, then I was out. When I passed out, I remember instantly going into a free fall while being in total darkness.

While free-falling, I felt trapped in a void in time, suspended, no dreams, no conscious awareness, total and absolute darkness. I was told the room quickly filled with twelve to fourteen nurses, CNAs, and doctors, all frantically working on me to regain my breathing. While all this was happening as I was passed out and free-falling, I could hear the conversations going on around me. Gloria later told me one doctor called for the crash wagon, but they gave him excuses as to why they couldn't come now. Whatever he said to the person on the phone, they came immediately. I again had to be placed on a respirator to stay alive; my breathing had stopped, and my organs became septic. Interesting side note, sepsis is the body's extreme response to an infection. Infections leading to sepsis most often start in the lungs. According to the CDC, the cause of the infection starts before a patient goes to the hospital in almost 87 percent of cases. Over 1.7 million adults in America develop sepsis (Prescott, Posa, and Dantes 2023).

I was administered an extremely potent antiviral that, in my opinion, eradicates every bacterium and virus in the body. I regained consciousness in a day or two, and the doctor was there by my bed when I woke up. He said to me, "I didn't think I would see those eyes ever open again." He further explained I had developed pneumonia from vomiting and aspirating, filling my lungs with particles of food. He thought I must have had some infection looming in my body prior to this that led to the process of the organs becoming septic, which led me to stop breathing. I had coded (code blue) and was placed on life support. My family was called in, but I survived. The next day, I was told I wasn't getting sufficient oxygen into my lungs, and they needed to install a trach. This requires a surgical procedure where an incision is made in the front of the neck and a breathing tube is placed into the trachea or windpipe.

Following the procedure, I was in a lot of pain and it hurt like hell to swallow. Plus, I was unable to talk. No one was able to read my lips; I don't know if that was unintentional or intentional? The pain persisted when swallowing for several more days and I was starting to develop a rawness in my throat that was very uncomfortable, almost unbearable. They kept insisting I needed to cough up the phlegm in my lungs. I tried to be compliant, but I was in a lot of pain, so very painful…I coughed as much as I could to produce the mucus. I still needed a lot of phlegm to be suctioned because I was unable to cough up enough, no matter how hard I tried. Finally, after fighting the pain in my throat and my inability to cough up the mucus, I had had enough. They were also pushing mass quantities of oxygen into my lungs to increase my capacity of blood oxygen. I was at the end of my rope.

I was quickly reaching my saturation point with everything hitting simultaneously. My food intake was liquid being pushed through a tube in my nose through to my stomach. That coupled with pneumonia and the tracheotomy (trach) with the stitches around the trach ring sewn in my neck along with all the beeping and lights—I had had enough! I told the doctor I wanted the trach removed. I couldn't take it anymore. He told me if they removed the trach, I wouldn't be able to breathe. I insisted on its removal. I wanted it out, now! Unbeknownst to me, there were hurdles that needed to be jumped before they could remove it.

For some reason when the trach was surgically placed in my throat, the gasket was not just placed in the incision but was stitched into the incision. Those stitches were becoming inflamed and infected—just what I needed. So, one of the nurses was allowed to remove the stitches without me taking any medication. Ouch! (It hurt so good, no not ever.) Well, I guess I had worn out my welcome in ICU, so as soon as a room was available, I was moved out of ICU. The monitoring and the weaning process was to begin to see if I could qualify for the trach to be removed.

Following five days of being closely and continuously monitored, I was given the good news by the pulmonologist that I was cleared to have the trach removed. I sure was a happy camper. I could have jumped out of bed to do the happy dance. Unfortunately, I had lost all the progress I'd made in regaining strength and endurance to walk. This setback forced me to start physical therapy all over again. Remember, every setback is followed by a comeback.

Attempt number three to leave and return home.

I knew for sure I would not be returning to the nursing facility but would be going to Saint Luke's Rehabilitation Hospital. I was hopeful I would be able to finish the program there before my insurance ran out, then go home. It seemed this time was different. With every thought of going to physical therapy, I attracted more worry and anxiety, causing me to become hypervigilant. After starting physical therapy, it came to me the reason for all the surge of emotions. As a result of several setbacks, I was becoming hypersensitive to exertion. A belief I have used many times came to me: "Control your thoughts that control your emotions, then you can control your actions." So, I had to override negative emotions in my recovery. It took time, just like swimming upstream takes longer and is a lot harder than swimming downstream.

Toward the end of October 2021, I had returned to Saint Luke's Rehab Hospital. I knew we wouldn't be starting at ground zero, but the climb was going to be difficult. I was motivated to push myself to get to the level of functioning to go home, please and thank you. My progress through therapy went well without glitches or setbacks. I completed physical therapy on November 18, 2021, and was released the next day to return home.

Finally, after being hospitalized for 144 days, I returned home. The entire ride home seemed like I was in constant prayer and meditation. It hadn't hit home, I never thought I would see this day, I was so very grateful and blessed. My daughters surprised me by having the Christmas tree up and decorated when I arrived. What a wonderful blessing. Thank you, wonderful and beautiful daughters. Love you.

In many studies it is well documented that physical functioning improves with heart transplantation. Yet, the literature continues to be dominated by descriptive studies, with few attempts to test interventions to optimize physical functioning outcomes, namely whether physical functioning gains differ by sex. But with continuous flow devices, women's small body surface area made technology less accessible to them (Rosenberger et al. 2012).

EXERCISING AND RECOVERY

I found one study of a small sample of randomized controlled trial patients that yielded promising results regarding the potential of exercise training interventions in populations that examined physical capacity and QOL (Quality of Life) in bridge-to-transplant patients. Patients who either completed an eight-week cardiovascular and strength training program in conjunction with a home walking program or the walking program alone. By the end of the study, both groups had experienced significant improvements in exercise capacity and QOL, with the exercise training group showing trends toward relatively greater improvements. The goal of this study was to evaluate physical and psychological factors in heart transplant patients. The physical symptoms, psychological complaints, and limitations of patients were compared at the time of admission to the waiting list, as well as one- and five-years following heart transplantation, using a prospective design. The study involved thirty-three patients (thirty males and three females). When they were admitted, their average age was forty-eight. Of them, two had valvular insufficiency, eight had coronary heart disease, and twenty-three had cardiomyopathy. (Rosenberger et al. 2012; Martin et al. 2009).

These individuals were unable to move about freely; engage in sports, hobbies, or gardening; have sex; work; or eat when they were admitted due to heart failure symptoms. More than 74 percent of participants reported having moderate to poor physical and mental health. They struggled with emotional issues including anxiety, despair, restlessness, low self-worth, low drive, and low self-esteem. At the end of therapy (four to eight weeks after the operation), all physical and mental symptoms, including restrictions, were significantly reduced ($p < 0.0001$ to $p < 0.001$), with the exception of trembling, numbness in the hands and feet, and trouble eating. A year following surgery, patients reported even less physical complaints ($p < 0.01$). Seventy-four percent said they were in good or outstanding physical and emotional health. Five years post-operatively—in contrast to physical status, restrictions, and physical complaints—the emotional complaints had increased significantly. Patients reported excellent physical performance up to five years post-operatively. On the other hand, the study revealed their emotional well-being had significantly deteriorated from one to five years postoperatively. Attention should, therefore, not only be paid to the good physical health of the survivors, but also to the worsening of their emotional status (Bunzel and Laederach-Hofmann 2000).

You will work with occupational and physical therapists to increase your strength and endurance. When discharged from the hospital, they will advise you on the safest and healthiest ways to increase your level of exercise. Your transplant dietician will teach you and your caregivers about healthy eating habits connected to different facets of your posttransplant well-being. If needed or requested a mental health specialist will engage with you and your family members to discuss coping mechanisms for this new phase of life and reintegration.

SIDEBAR ON AGING AND GROWING OLD

We take growing older for granted because we believe it won't happen to us. People in ancient Rome only survived into their thirties, which was attributed to a higher birth death rate, illness, and warfare. Our life expectancy has undoubtedly increased due to modern medicine and lifestyle choices including diet, exercise, and medication. But hold on; researchers have studied the ancient remains from Cholula, Mexico, and discovered most of the individuals were older than fifty. Average life expectancy has increased as a result of contemporary technology and medicine, which has enabled humans to survive from birth through childhood, into adulthood. Recall that becoming older is a blessing because not everyone has the opportunity to live their best years.

Another unfounded belief about becoming older is you need less sleep. The truth is humans require six to eight hours of sleep per night, a requirement that only changes throughout the growing and developmental stages of life, when children and adolescents require more energy to develop. We need the same amount of sleep after our twenties as we need for the rest of our lives. Many of us are taught to think as we get older, we don't need as much sleep. As a result of illness, discomfort, pharmaceutical side effects, and frequent urination, the majority of older people actually suffer from sleep deprivation and have poor quality sleep when they do. To feel refreshed, a nice afternoon power nap is usually in order.

The Oxford Dictionary defines "recovery" as "a return to a normal state, mind, or strength; the action or process of recovering custody or control of something stolen or lost." This description is interesting to me. However, I found another definition I believe is more appropriate for my needs: a transformative process that helps people live more autonomous lives, enhance their health and wellness, and work toward realizing their full potential. Now, that phrase captures the essence of my journey and my healing (Substance Abuse and Mental Health Services Administration 2012).

Lesson in Resilience: I learned during recovery that patience and endurance run in tandem. Patience in most things is a prerequisite; waiting for the right moment is essential. Endurance must persist through the challenges that arise along the way, not surrendering to circumstances. Ponder this for a moment: If you start today, imagine where you'll be next week, end of the month, and end of the year. If you don't start today, think where you'll be in a week, in a month, and in a year. Where you are versus where you could be. What are you waiting for? You can't buy more time—now what?

CHAPTER 12

Emotional Toll of the Journey

"Learn to forget what has hurt you, without forgetting what it taught you."

—NORM BOUCHARD

I experienced multiple trips on my emotional roller coaster that took me through hell then to heaven, several times. Which do I prefer?

Stanford Medicine's Health Care website states, "Up to 50 percent of patients with advanced cardiac disease experience anxiety or depression. Following a transplant, 63 percent of heart recipients develop anxiety and/or depression during the first posttransplant year (2023). Along with emotional distress, there is an increased risk of cognitive impairment, generally caused by lowered cardiac output and poor blood flow. Medications may increase the level of cognitive impairment.

For the entirety of this journey, the struggle has not been the surgery or numerous procedures or the medicine or the doctors or staff, it's been the endless loop of mental volleyball that constantly slides along the continuum of emotions. The continuum moving from the extremes of overconfidence involving superpowers to sliding all the way to the other end filled with total doubt, doom, and gloom. The enigma is being stuck in the continuous endless loop filled mostly with doubt and worry. In other words, the entire journey has been an inside game of self-regulation of thoughts to try to diminish fear and contribute to increased strength, peace, and gratitude. Always striving to find the sweet spot of this endless journey and to find ways to put my trust in the team of nurses, doctors, and most of all, God.

To illustrate my point, I remember a couple times, early into posttransplant when I was hooked up to monitoring equipment with alerts. My heart monitor alarm suddenly went off, the nurses rushed into the room in response. They said with urgency, "You're in A-fib." I knew the next step was for them to call the doctor to report, and the doctor would order a procedure to shock my heart back into rhythm or order medication to be administered in an IV drip. The medicine would either put me back in rhythm or it would require surgery to shock my heart into rhythm.

I didn't want or need either of these remedies, so I thought I would give meditation a try, the least invasive of the other two procedures. I believed in and practiced meditation for most of my adult life. So, I asked the nurse to give me twenty or thirty minutes alone so I could have a chance to manage the problem. I went into my mind, deeply listening to my respiration. I went into a deep, relaxing meditation. Then I focused on my heartbeat, slowing my breathing and slowing my heartbeat. Twenty or thirty minutes later, I could tell, and I knew I had slowed my heart rate back to normal. Within moments, the nurse came back into my room and asked, "What did you do?"

During pretransplant and posttransplant, I experienced surges of anger and surges of deep depression and crying that led me to becoming very emotional. When I realized the absurdity of this range of emotions in my first episode of stewing and wallowing in self-pity, I broke out in laughter. I stopped for a moment to understand the why of it all. I felt attacked and victimized at the same time. I caught myself before falling too far and changed my thoughts from negative; I was able to laugh and free up my emotions. I learned I could counter my emotions by consciously letting go and taking charge of how I wanted to feel. I am free and no longer at the mercy of people, their actions, or their responses—no longer a victim. Additionally, I came to realize over the years I had accumulated a trash compactor of negative feelings, attitudes, and beliefs I needed to confront and resolve.

As for the results of my introspection, I found for most of my life when I encountered situations that were filled with raw emotions, I either suppressed, escaped, or stood my ground (freeze, flight, or fight) my feelings. I learned along the way to try not to internalize negative or sad feelings. I could have easily taken the route of using alcohol or narcotics, but instead I found sports and work as my escape route. During my first encounter of heart issues when facing my own mortality, I inadvertently went (in my mind) to my Zen Garden to neutralize my emotions. I was desperate to stay unconscious and not allow any awareness of inner thoughts and feelings.

When looking in the rearview mirror of life, I recalled many times of living amid denial and many long-standing problems continually cropped into my consciousness, mainly regarding relationships and the inability to find contentment and fulfillment in my life. I had an unquenchable desire for peace and contentment, but it was like trying to grab air in your hand, not having the ability to taste any of the satisfactions of life, the repeated haunting of seeing the finish line ahead but never being able to reach it. I had the mindset of it was never enough and never good enough, wanting more-more-more.

Over the weeks and months while in the hospital, many thoughts came into my awareness, thoughts to be truth. All thoughts were the result of a life of accumulated negative feelings. As I noted each of these limiting thoughts and feelings, I began to write each of them off. I made a list of each feeling that came into my consciousness and crossed it off, then practiced thought blocking. I noticed that I then had to change my intentions. I had to change from "I won't," "I can't," and "I will not," to "I will," "I am willing," "I might," and "I am blessed that I am able." I experienced an unleashing or unchaining of emotions that allowed me to open up to be at peace knowing everything will be as it was meant to be.

I knew my negative or misguided thoughts and feelings blocked many situations, which resulted in outcomes I wished to avoid. When we allow things to unfold naturally, instead of fighting (tugging, pulling, pushing, or dragging) the current, we waste valuable energy, which in turn causes ripples in possible future positive outcomes. No, I don't want you to sit there and do nothing, on the contrary. I learned that most of the time I was too scared to do anything, but I taught myself to then do it scared, do it anyway. Go ahead and ask yourself all the questions, do your due diligence. Allow the natural flow of things as well as you can and enjoy the beautiful outcomes.

After reading many articles and talking with patients about medical trauma, I find it is normal for family and patients to feel a wide range of emotions during the transplant journey, and yes, I concur. One phrase I heard repeatedly was, "Every person recovers differently." Not everyone progresses at the same rate. In the following couple of paragraphs are suggestions from helping professionals who have shown success with their processes. The first lists the essential ways to cope, the second lists stressors of social interactions and relationships that may be encountered, and last are ways to learn to accept a new way of life following trauma or transplant.

I think it is essential to learn ways to cope with uncertainty. If you don't, it will become your norm, at least for a time. I think it is also essential to have emotional awareness and to learn emotional regulation. Both are a learned process (Robinson and Smith 2023).

1. Pay attention to how you feel, or when you start feeling stressed or scared. What do you notice in your body? Or in your mind?
2. It is important to name the emotion you are feeling. Does this emotion fit with the physical feelings you noticed?

3. Is this emotion acceptable? If so, just allow it to be and ride it out?

4. What need is this emotion alerting you to? Anxiety might mean you need some reassurance or a sense of safety. Sadness, you need comfort. Anger may suggest you need to put up a boundary. Important to learn: worry doesn't need to accompany anxiety.

5. Do a feelings check-in regularly. What feelings do I notice? What do I need? What can I do right now about it? Might be to just allow it; it depends.

Social and relationship stressors that may be experienced during the journey:

- Loss of control over your life
- Lack of support from family and friends
- Feeling isolated and alone, like no one else understands
- Financial problems
- Feeling helpless and dependent on others.

Radical acceptance once experiencing a life changing event:

Acceptance takes time. Dr. Kristin Neff identified five stages in coming to full acceptance, learning to accept your new reality and not resist.

Resist – struggle against the reality, if you will, "swimming upstream." But this is a natural response to change.

Exploring – Ability to turn to discomfort with vigor and willingness.

Tolerating – I don't like this a bit, but I will grit my teeth and will tolerate.

Allowing – Ambivalence of feeling, letting them come and go.

Befriending – Learning to value and learn difficult emotions. Learning to endure difficult emotions (Neff 2012).

Even though above I suggested ways to cope, ways to counter social and relational stressors, and ways to adapt to a new way of life, I want to include ways to keep a clearer perception in the midst of it all.

Susan Dunn has done much research and reports on her website ten barriers to clear perception when tangled with emotions (2013).

Your vision becomes clear and is self-evident if you have high emotional intelligence and are good at reality testing. If your emotions cloud your thinking, you become stuck in the past, inflexible, inauthentic, or inept at verbal and nonverbal communication, alas, everything is not self-evident.

When you develop your emotional intelligence, and the ability to understand and manage your emotions and those of others, you see things clearly. You can avoid the following pitfalls to accurate perception and smart choices:

1. How you wish things were.
2. How you think things should be.
3. Believing that how things have always been in the past is the way they are now, and ever will be.

4. Assumptions about situations in-the-moment which seem at the surface level to be similar to experiences and people in the past. Assumptions always need to be checked out.

5. Your persona or inauthentic, unintegrated self, which shifts according to mood, emotion, person, and situation, leaving you without compass or anchor.

6. Your ability to delude yourself because of lack of self-knowledge.

7. Self-sabotaging because of lack of self-knowledge, self-management, and low EQ.

8. Fear, anger, jealousy, and other strong emotions distort thinking.

9. Hearing what you want to hear or need to hear instead of what's being said. Failing to consider the other 10. And the other person's nonverbal behavior.

10. Distortion from relying on other people's perceptions of reality and/or "catching" their emotions.

In sum, we are our emotions. They influence our perception of reality. The more you understand yourself and your own emotions, the better you can understand their effect upon your perceptions of reality and manage them so you can make smart choices.

Self-Sabotage—Avoid throwing in the towel. As humans, our thoughts create havoc that leads to those feelings that cause us to add unsuitable behaviors to evoke fight, flight, or freeze responses. Inner dialogue causes our feelings that dictate stress and anxieties, resulting in suffering and added turmoil. It is our attachment to these thoughts that cause us suffering. Let go of these thoughts, allow them to pass, avoiding control or attachment to them (Dunn 2013).

Lesson in Resilience: You have the power to create your future. Only you control your thoughts, feelings, and behaviors. Don't allow your negative emotions to rule your thoughts. Conceive and achieve, you are your thoughts.

From a Caregiver Perspective—Living in the Trenches

"To make a difference in someone's life, you don't have to be brilliant, rich, beautiful, or perfect. You just have to care."

—MANDY HALE

The worldwide heart transplant survival rate for adults is greater than 85 percent after one year and 69 percent after five years according to the Newark Beth Israel Heart Transplant team (RWJBarnabas Health n.d.). Most people eventually return to their normal activities after a heart transplant. Survival rates continue to improve, especially when the recipient is blessed with an outstanding caregiver.

By the time this book hits publication, it will be more than two years posttransplant, and for that entire time, I owe my recovery to a wonderful, selfless, gives-all caregiver Gloria Benedict. I'm active and healthy, making good choices on food intake, exercising daily, and getting good sleep. Developing a healthy routine or regiment is essential. I heard my granddaddy tell someone, "You'll never get serious with life and do the right things to take good care of yourself until you develop a terminal/chronic illness." I now know that to be the truth.

By June 28, 2021, I had known Gloria for just over two years. I thought I knew her deepest thoughts and most of her desires. However, until that fateful day when I made "that call" to tell her I was headed to the hospital and the news wasn't going to be good, she showed me there is so much more to her than I could have ever imagined. The following days and months revealed a depth of caregiving and attunement I had never known before.

Gloria describes the following from her viewpoint as my caregiver.

"I called Jim's daughters to let them know what was happening. By the time I arrived at the hospital, Jim was already in surgery. While I waited, my thoughts swirled with all the possible outcomes from his surgery. Afterward, he spent a few days in the hospital and then was released to go home. Both Jim and I were afraid of his being released so soon. We simply agreed he wasn't ready to be out on his own yet. And as things unfolded, we were right.

"After Jim returned home, I was out of town visiting family, so he was by himself. While returning home from my visit, Jim was calling me—from the back of an ambulance that was taking him to the Heart Institute at Saint Luke's on the Plaza. A friend initially took Jim to Saint Luke's East emergency room, but they quickly determined he was in heart failure again. His condition was so critically grave they needed to transport him to the Heart Institute immediately. As soon as I arrived home, I was on my way to the hospital again. I found my way to the cardiac intensive care unit, which was a real gut punch that opened my eyes to the seriousness of Jim's condition.

"As Jim's continued health challenge emerged with all its uncertainties and unknowns, I began to feel the physical and emotional drain. So many thoughts and feelings bubbled up when I reflected on this very uncertain journey. Jim always kept a very positive attitude through it all, and I tried to always present with a positive posture for him as well. I think we were both too afraid to be anything else. He let it go to God. I didn't really have that luxury, but I did try desperately to stay positive. In retrospect, I wish I had journaled about the ebb and flow of each day. I think that would have been very therapeutic.

"As the weeks and months passed, I continued to get deeper into the daily grind and routine of it all. My world seemed to be a whirlwind of juggling all the balls of everyday living as well as Jim's health challenges. Not only taking care of my responsibilities but Jim's as well, paying bills, watering plants, cleaning the house, picking up mail and responding to it, doing his laundry. My world was spinning faster and faster, and at times overwhelmed me.

"I continued to go to work every day, where life was familiar and normal. Every day after work, I would go to the hospital to see Jim, and we would visit and talk about making plans for the future. We enjoyed each other's company and tried not to dwell too much on how our lives had been derailed. We knew it was only temporary, and we would be back on track before too long. These visits were very therapeutic for both of us. The doctors and nurses were very attentive to both our needs whenever I visited. I always received an in-depth report on Jim's condition and progress. After each visit, phone calls and texting were an everyday occurrence among Jim's daughters and friends, keeping everyone apprised of his ever-changing condition.

"Jim and I were blindsided by this journey. As I walked with him on this medical roller coaster, the days flew by. The doctors told us they were not able to save his heart. Jim's heart no longer functioned effectively, and he was placed on the transplant list. While Jim waited for a new heart, the doctors decided to install a heart pump to keep him alive. The pump would keep Jim alive, but not for more than fourteen days. A flood of emotions rushed in—fear, worry, anxiety, angst, concern. A heart had to be found!

"After the pump was installed, Jim had to remain lying flat on his back. He was not allowed to sit up at all. This was yet another heart-wrenching time to witness him endure. But he did…without complaint. His desire to live was so strong he would do whatever was required…he just chose life at every turn. Then the night came that we all wished and prayed for but didn't know if it would ever come…but it did. All the staff who were on duty came into Jim's room one after another with big smiles on their faces. It didn't register at first, but then it was spoken, "a heart has been found, a match." There are absolutely no words to express the joy that was bursting that night.

"There were so many ups and downs from the moment Jim was in recovery after the transplant until he progressed to physical therapy, a couple of times an emotional roller coaster for sure. Being at his side witnessing his struggles to gain his strength after being laid up for so long was particularly difficult for me. Jim was and is a very proud man who could always do anything. Watching him with limitations was hard. His perseverance paid off. When his insurance coverage for Saint Luke's was exhausted, it was decided that Jim would continue his physical therapy at a skilled nursing facility. Nobody really wanted this, but the insurance company was calling the shots. Jim was transferred to the facility, and it was awful to see him there in a room that did not meet ADA (American Disabilities Act) guidelines. More importantly, the facility was short-staffed. Nonetheless, Jim was determined to do what was necessary to survive. He was committed to recovery. He did all the therapy. Then there was another setback in store for him. He woke violently ill one night and was transported back to Saint Luke's Hospital. He was diagnosed with pneumonia, and his organs began to fail due to sepsis. The roller-coaster was taking off again.

"I really don't know how many times Jim was at death's door… too many, I suspect. I recall one frightening episode when I was visiting with Jim one afternoon. As we were talking, Jim wasn't responsive, and I wondered what was wrong. A nurse came into the room to give him a breathing treatment and he seemed not to like that, like he was fighting it. Then suddenly, his oxygen level was too low. Within seconds, his room was flooded with nurses, doctors, technicians—probably ten to twelve professionals. They were all working feverishly to keep Jim alive. The doctor was yelling orders. I will never forget one of the staff was phoning for some sort of equipment to be brought to Jim's room and she was informed that they were unable to bring the equipment for some reason. She was telling Jim's doctor when he raised his voice, 'Give me the phone, give me the phone.'

"He yelled into the phone that his patient was crashing, and they better get that machine to his room right now. I felt hysterical; I thought I was about to witness Jim die, and I was devastated. Then, in what seemed to be slow motion, the doctor turned to me to explain that Jim wasn't really going to die—he just had to say that to get the equipment he needed to the room as soon as possible. He told me not to worry. I was frantic and in tears. Another doctor explained that a trach had to be put in so that Jim would be able to breathe. My heart was so broken at the thought of Jim going through that again. How he hated that trach. I was told that they had no choice. It had to be done if he was to survive. I cried and called his daughters. As a bystander, watching a loved one fight for survival takes an emotional toll that cannot be effectively described in words, only felt. I felt totally helpless, unable to do anything except let my emotions run out of control.

"Jim finally came home for good on November 19, 2021. He had been in the hospital and rehab since June 28. I moved into his home to help him during the transition period. He still used a walker and received in-home physical therapy two to three times a week. We were adjusting to all his meds and keeping track of his vitals. We were just so happy for him to be home. We had never lived together before, so there were adjustments. But it was all good, and I was happy I could be there for him. I think his anxiety subsided a bit having me there. There was still a lot of work to keep it all going.

"Now that we are on the other side of this traumatic event, I take a step back and reflect. I can see during this entire period I was flooded with old clinging emotions from when my sister was dying of cancer, my mom dealing with dementia, and my father dying while in a nursing home from medical complications. The entire tsunami of emotions continued to rush over me, mixing with the emotions I was experiencing with Jim plus bringing forth all my past traumas of life, as if I carried an additional weight on my shoulders. At the time, I hadn't realized the breakdown of emotions or why I felt such a heavy burden. I don't know how I made it through it all.

"Having been on this journey with Jim, I now find that so many of the nightmarish thoughts and memories are moving into the dark recesses of my memory. Choosing to live life to the fullest every day now is the number one priority. Jim and I are going forward with a positive, healthy lifestyle. We are immensely grateful for the wonderful opportunity to live, unleashed!"

You just read from a caregiver perspective; now I want to share an example of surviving a catastrophic illness void of a caregiver, after surviving a transplant and returning home. It was January 2022, and I contracted COVID while at home. I called the cardio team and reported my symptoms. I was told not to go to the emergency room. With my compromised immunity, going to the emergency room would only increase my risk and exposure to additional sickness, viruses, and bacteria, and the only treatment options available were

Tylenol and Mucinex. I remained in bed at home for a total of six weeks struggling to breathe, and every time I stood up, I became dizzy and light-headed, on the verge of passing out.

So again, I'm flat on my back in bed, struggling to breathe, weak, and dizzy, with no one here to help me with nutrition or safety. I became ever vigilant when getting out of bed and moving around the house, especially since I was at a high risk of falling. What is it they say? "Only the strong survive," a mantra for my entire life. As my distressed breathing and symptoms somewhat subsided, I wanted to start up with physical therapy again. My challenge this time—dizziness. I worried these symptoms would be with me for my remaining days. At this point, the only way I could possibly move around was with the assistance of a walker.

Once again, I was at the bottom of the mountain ready to start my climb to the top. I fought the urge to lose hope and quit, to settle for being in a wheelchair for the rest of my life—not good. This time was unique compared to the two previous setbacks; this time I struggled with breathing. I was unable to take in enough oxygen. It felt as though I constantly gasped for air. The lightheadedness and losing my balance continued. I feared this would become my new "normal." Talk about adding fear and worry. Here, my superpowers kicked in my mantra at this point: "Ain't no stopping me now." March 24, 2022, I completed my second round of in-home physical therapy. I love setbacks, not ever. Around the first of April, I started outpatient therapy at Saint Luke's East, for the third time.

Following the preceding episode of another life-threating illness, I am now, more than ever, so grateful Gloria was my angel during this entire roller-coaster challenge of life. She was steadfast by my side, enduring any and all occurrences and able to push through the many days and weeks with little or no prospect of success. With no end in sight, she stayed and conquered. Thank you, Gloria. It would have been a lonely journey without you…many blessings.

It would be very remiss of me to not mention my daughters, who are both RNs who oversaw all my medical care. Without their love, care, and medical expertise along with doctor collaboration, I would not have made it through the challenging storms. Thank you, love you both. Many thanks and blessings to your grandmother and aunt: both were nurses who led you to follow in their footsteps. Couldn't have made it through without you.

Here is another caregiver perspective I wanted to share.

JANE'S CAREGIVER STORY

After talking with Jim about my own experiences as a caregiver, he asked me to write a couple of paragraphs for his book. What follows are the experiences I encountered while being the primary caregiver for my mother.

In April of 2016, mother came to live with me after having lived with my younger sister for several years. My sister needed a break, and I agreed mother would come stay with me for several months. My relationship with mother had always been confrontational, but I also knew my sister desperately needed a break. So, mother came to stay for a while, but ended up staying until she passed.

Caring for an aging parent, while altruistic, proved too much for me to handle. So, we found an assisted living facility where mother could maintain some level of independence. But even then, the doctor visits, dispensing medication, and purchasing supplies fell to me. At the time, I also worked a full-time job. I did as much as I could to help defray the cost of the facility. I purchased an automatic medication dispenser, the kind you could program to turn to allow you to take the pills out of. That little device worked very well. I could put up to fourteen days' worth of medications in it, and the alarm would notify mother it was time to take her meds.

One morning, the phone rang with her special ring and picture. I was on my way to work. Mother said, "I can't get my medication out of the machine." So, I turned the car around, headed back home, got her medications and the key to the dispenser, then went to her place. When I arrived, she was agitated. Upon looking at the machine, she had been trying to get her evening medications out. Informing her of this, she argued it had just gone off and she couldn't get her medications. However, looking on the counter, I noticed one pill standing on its edge. I surmised she had turned the device over but missed her hand as I found the rest of the pills on the floor.

Several months later, the facility informed us she needed more care than I could provide. So, they took over dispensing her medication.

Eventually, even that was short-lived as her health continued to decline. Summer of 2019, hospice entered the picture and relieved me of even the few things I continued doing for mother. She remained in hospice until she passed away in January 2020. Losing mother left an empty place in my life, but I am thankful she never had to endure what followed in March 2020. Being a caregiver was both a gift I could give my mother and a drain on me both physically and emotionally. I am in awe of those who do it for years on end, like my mother did for my dad after his stroke.

When researching "challenges of a caregiver" I found a lot of varying opinions, but the following summarizes the main areas or challenges that I repeatedly came across:

1. Caregiver burnout must top the list of challenges as a caregiver. Working a full-time job in addition to caregiver responsibilities is extremely time intensive.
2. Financial strain falls on the shoulders of caregivers. The position is unpaid and often expenses fall on the shoulders of the one providing care.
3. Isolation is ongoing since the time requirements don't stop. It is difficult to place the person being cared for second to the caregiver's other activities.

I'm so grateful that Gloria was my angel during this time, and especially for both my daughters, Taia and Ashley, for walking with me during all the tough hospital time and decisions. Today, some two years and five months posttransplant, I think I'm doing exceptionally well, considering where I was and where I am today. Can you spell blessed with me now? I'm able to function as a normal adult. I can get in and out of bed, shower, and use the restroom. I make all my meals and go to the grocery store to purchase food. I clean my home, do my laundry, fold it, and put it away. I try to go to the gym three to five times a week, depending on my schedule. My vitals are in normal range. My medications are minimal: Tacrolimus, sirolimus, Synthroid, lovastatin, eighty milligrams aspirin, tamsulosin, and essential vitamins and minerals. I am blessed, I am grateful, and living a life of go-see-do.

> **_Lesson in Resilience:_** Some are blind and can't see. Thomas Edison saw incandescent light before the first electric bulb ever glowed. It is important to have a clear vision that is filled with hope with goals in sight. Belief, filled with hope, gives one a clear vision. You must have hope to have a goal, and you must have a goal to have hope.

CHAPTER 14

Importance of Good Physical Condition

Upon entering the hospital on June 28, 2021, I weighed 258 pounds. I had ignored the fact I was in the worst physical condition I'd been in for the past twenty years. Shamefully, I had not worked out at a gym or done any aerobic exercise for over three years. My diet consisted of lots of sweet, iced tea, fatty red meats, starches, and one or two cocktails most evenings. It seemed I was always tired, but more exhausted, which I accepted as my new normal. I can't remember the last time I had six to eight hours of quality, restful sleep. I woke up in the mornings tired and went to bed tired. I always found myself either dragging or drooping. The only way I made it through an entire day was to rely on a constant adrenaline rush. I found I had to mentally push myself, get pumped to literally push the adrenaline to excite my brain to wake up.

By three thirty in the afternoon, I frequently crashed and burned, which forced me to come home for a one-to-two-hour nap. On days I was so busy that I couldn't take a nap, I had to push through the valley of slumberland and bring on the adrenaline rush, exciting the adrenal glands, in turn increasing my heart rate to get my blood flowing. I relied on lots of caffeinated coffee in those days. Gee, why would I have heart problems? Most days I would have been perfectly fine staying in bed all day. Plus, I hadn't seen a doctor in over five years—can you spell *borrowed time* with me? I knew deep inside I was becoming ill, but I was too afraid to see a doctor since it had been so long. I didn't want to hear any bad news, really, or should I say not hear the truth. When it came to medical, I was groomed to think terminal and worst-case scenario.

Since my premature birth, Mom was overprotective, almost to the point of paranoid. Growing up, I was very confused about my health. Sometimes I felt I was being convinced that I was a sickly kid or even worse a Munchausen by proxy kid. Remembering back to the age of seven, it seemed as though I was at the doctor's office weekly. Since I was born prematurely and the added trauma of Stuart dying at seven days old, Mom had ramped up the protection mode to hyper alert. I learned fear and apprehension of doctors, nurses, and staff because of the constant prodding or testing for some suspected illness.

If I had known the early warning signs of heart issues before it went into crisis mode, I could have learned the prerequisites of being in shape before surgery. Prehabilitation is a way of improving postoperative outcomes. This is becoming increasingly recommended prior to a wide range of scheduled surgeries with stats to prove less recovery time and increased performance, lowering postoperative risks. The successful outcome of surgery depends not only on the doctor and medical staff but also what the patient does weeks prior to surgery.

These factors contribute to the likelihood of the patient returning to a physically and psychologically healthy lifestyle. The hope is with prehabilitation, the patient will have a higher functioning capacity with higher tolerance and quicker bounce back. Even though, according to Calland et al., one month following an operation death occurs in less than 8 percent of transplant patients. Hoping to drive this number down by increasing the physical endurance through a steady regimen of exercise, it has been noted that fitness levels are a strong predictor of postoperative risk. Even as little as two weeks of exercise prior to surgery reduces risk and increases healthier outcomes for the patient (Calland et al. 2002).

When the doctors determined I needed a new heart, they first completed an in-depth assessment to find out more about my health to check for any underlying problems, which would affect my being a suitable candidate for a transplant.

Several major tests needed to be performed to determine risk factors. Many blood tests to check for infections and organ function— chest X-rays, lung functioning, a CT scan, an ultrasound to assess kidney function, a cardiac catheterization and a coronary angiograph, a special X-ray to look inside the heart, and an electrocardiogram (EKG) to measure electrical activity of my heart.

The doctors mentioned some health factors could rule me out for a transplant, for example:

1. If damage to any organ was found
2. If an active infection was found.
3. If cancer was found, it needed to be treated first.
4. If I had damaged blood vessels because of diabetes or high cholesterol.
5. Obesity, alcohol abuse, nicotine addiction, are major roadblocks that would postpone surgery.
6. Age is not a factor when determining whether transplant is suitable but is rarely performed on people over the age of sixty-eight due to other health issues making a transplant too risky. Most have the "check engine light" come on.

If possible, transplant patients should initiate an exercise routine prior to surgery. Preoperative interventions, such as prehabilitation with the aim to improve patients' physical, metabolic, and psychosocial capacities in preparation for surgery, are recommended.

Diet and nutrition are essential for success in both pre- and posttransplant patients. Dietary restrictions are deemed necessary to offset the side effects from medication. I was placed on a type llA hyperlipoproteinemia (300 milligrams cholesterol) diet, that consisted of no concentrated sweets and low-sodium restriction, ten to twelve ounces of water daily. Sleep and relaxation, I believe, is the utmost important activity for you to complete nightly. It affects so many bodily functions that can put the body out of whack (Quint et al. 2023).

I believe nature heals and nature contact is a must to our survival. Just a walk in the woods or a stroll by the beach on a sunny morning can awaken the innermost feelings of happiness and peace, and environmental psychology has gone a long way proving this fact. Our attraction toward nature is part of our soul, is genetic, and is deep-rooted in evolution.

For example, have you ever wondered why most people prefer to book an accommodation that has a great view from the balcony or the terrace? Why do patients who get a natural view from their hospital bed recover sooner than others? Or why does it happen that when stress takes a toll on our mind, we crave time to figure things out amid nature? Frank Lloyd Wright said, "Study Nature, love Nature, stay close to Nature. It will never fail you." Why do we feel so empowered when we are close to nature? What happens to us when the soft breeze or the warm sun touches us (Chowdhury 2019).

Lesson in Resilience: The body's capability to adapt to challenges, access stamina, find strength, and recover naturally is amazing. The ability to keep moving, even if it's a tiny step, especially when one is depressed or in terrible pain—this is physical resilience. Don't stop, don't give up, keep moving.

CHAPTER 15

Discovering Life's Sweet Spot

"To live is the rarest thing in the world. Most people exist, that is all"

—OSCAR WILDE

Stand for something or fall for anything. Find your passion in your life and career. Passionate participation in life today is all you ever have; this is your life. Are you living who you want to be?

Psychosocial outcomes and quality of life (QOL) are important indicators of the success of heart transplantation and mechanical circulatory support (MCS). The literature has continued to identify correlators and predictors of psychosocial outcomes in five domains: physical functioning, psychological, behavioral, social functioning, and global QOL (Rosenberger et al. 2012). Researchers in France found attitude determines risk for dementia. When older adults were asked to rate their quality of life, researchers found a correlation of dementia.

Most people I've known saw their entire career as just a J-O-B that lacked passion and fulfillment. Most would agree their job was filled with much drudgery and regret. Most find their jobs undesirable and meaningless. Most jobs you wouldn't do voluntarily without numerical consideration. Gallup surveyed one million employees in sixty-six countries and asked them this question: "Do you get the chance to do what you do best at work every day?" Only one in five—a mere 20 percent—said yes (Clouet and Lai 2022).

Fallacy: when asked, most organizations assume anyone can excel in any job, provided they receive enough training and try hard enough. They take strengths for granted and try to fix weaknesses. This competency approach is a huge waste of energy, time, and money.

- Selection – the process must address what talents are needed to fill a position.
- Evaluation – a circular process that ends up going nowhere. Focus becomes what the person doesn't bring to their job, strengths taken for granted.
- Training – if it is not a strength or area of passion, employees have little interest or aptitude. Not good use of time.
- Role allocation – sifting and sorting people into the roles they will go on to perform in life.

The US Bureau of Labor Statistics reports that less than 2 percent of the workforce have "careers" (2023). Most took jobs that offered extrinsic rewards based on future growth or stability, with benefits that provided security for family and planning for the future. Some went to work or pursued careers that followed their parents' desires and footsteps. I think it is important to not get so wrapped up in a career busy making a living to forget to make a life. Please consider the possibility that if you die tonight, your employer will have your position filled by the weekend.

Few of us captured careers filled with desire, passion, and compassion, but rather out of necessity to survive. I talk with many people who are still working beyond retirement age out of necessity to survive. I have also noticed people who are retired are withdrawn from life, making their world smaller. I posit several reasons this is occurring; they include the loss of a spouse or family member or loss of a longtime friend. All of those reasons has led the majority of us down the path that results in the loss of zest and go-see-do attitudes.

Ponder this:

Work eight hours to live and enjoy four hours.
Work six days to enjoy one day off.
Work eight hours to eat in fifteen minutes.
Work eight hours to sleep five hours.
Work all year to take off two weeks.
Work thirty years to be able to retire and live for? (Fill in the blank.)

I think no matter what you do in life, it is vital to always and ever have the desire to finish the journey, to complete the walk, literally cross the finish line of life. Finish well; it is never too late to alter the direction you're headed in and leave with a fulfilled, task-accomplished smile on your face. I'm not saying to finish first but rather keep a healthy pace filled with commitment and intention until our last breath. It is important to develop clarity on what you stand for and the person you want to become. If you don't stand for something, you will fall for anything. Be true to yourself and stand tall to be yourself; it's not too late to become the person you were meant to be. Consider why you are still here? It's obvious you haven't completed what you were sent here to accomplish. Separation for preparation for the new me.

It is important to focus on acceptance and appreciation of where you are today and what you have accomplished in life, not on what you don't have. First, accept who you are today, all of you, everything good and bad about yourself, unconditional acceptance. Then you can love that person you become tomorrow. Learn to never be jealous or envious of others; it only builds resentment and animosity within you. In other words, always be grateful for what you do have and be grateful for what you don't have. Ponder that for a moment. Second, assess your emotional maturity. Value and realize everyone has an opinion: value others' opinions. If you do listen, you are open to learning something new or different. This is a daily must do.

Everyone has an opinion, a value difference. Think of opinions like the 360 degrees, vertically and horizontally infinite ways to view that ball. Remember, you can't change anyone. Save your energy; you will eventually need it somewhere that will make a difference. Listen and learn…don't constantly talk and spew purpose. You are probably one of plenty to join the ranks of people who didn't reach all their goals. Trust me, you are part of the majority, not the exception.

Now is the time to erase the past, leave it behind, and look in the direction you want to move forward and set new goals with strategies filled with purpose and passion. It doesn't mean you're finished; it means it's time to start a new season of your life, not out of necessity but out of passion and renewed purpose.

Find your passion by exploring what it is that you have always wanted to do, that if you were doing it, you would lose track of time and couldn't do it enough. You would never become bored or tired of doing it. Finding your sweet spot isn't about focusing solely on your strengths or your passion, but rather on fulfillment and deeper meaning. It takes a lot of courage to step out of where you're at and step into where you're supposed to be.

Stop looking in the rearview mirror where you've been; focus forward. For most of us, because of our own selfish desires, will never experience the sweet spot of life. This is a place where everything comes together and produces the best possible result with minimal effort. Maslow referred to this moment in time as self-actualized, resulting in deep satisfaction and fulfillment. It is when we engage in something outside of ourselves that we create deeper meaning and purpose that brings fulfillment and contentment in life, finding our sweet spot. Most have a desire to leave a legacy or significance in the world, "that we made a difference, a contributor" (Komninos 2020).

Remember, life is not guaranteed, life has good days, bad days, and terrible days. Embrace the good and great days, push through and get through the rough days; they too shall pass. Having meaning in life is when we have a connection to something larger. The people who have this in their lives have fewer mental and physical issues and lead a better quality of life.

Research has found meaningfulness comes from three resources: goal setting, spiritual connection, higher calling, and having a deep interconnection of intimacy to a spouse or kids or extended family and friends.

I find most of us are trapped in the vortex of failure. If you never hope for anything from life, you're never deceived. Most of the time, we stay stuck in the past, reflecting on distorted self-perception of what we have accomplished, and either embittered or with a delusional perception of self.

Most often we develop an external belief of the outside world—specifically identifying our boss, spouse, mother, father—finding someone to blame for our failure. I once read we spend much of our life "*shoulding* all over ourselves"; *I should have said this, I should have done this, I shouldn't have felt that way about her.*

I don't have time to wait. I can't make up time and I can't save time. Make the best use of your time; make it count.

I don't have time to be angry. Don't sweat the small things; at this stage, everything is small stuff.

I don't have time to leave things unsaid. Inability to inhibit.

I don't have time to blame others. In every transaction, we each have a share of responsibility; own it.

I don't have time to keep looking in the rearview mirror of life. We don't get redos but can change course of direction.

I don't have time to worry about what will happen. Live in the moment; it is when you have the most control and least stress.

Pure consciousness is a moment without thought, without feelings, only awareness is present, non-reflective. Your feelings and thoughts do not cling to anything, letting go, creating interior silence. Eventually, the more you practice this state of pure consciousness it becomes a normal state, delightful peace. Our lives consist of a three-dimensional world that is spiritually dim. When in pure consciousness, the world becomes four-dimensional, I am.

What brings you the most joy and fulfillment?

Discovering yourself or "uncovering yourself," self-discovery.

The majority of finding out where you want to finish life is assessing where you are now. Before that self-discovery can start, you will need to uncover self, who you truly are, "the man in the mirror" or the person you are when no one else is looking. It is essential to become transparent, being true to yourself, the person you truly are meant to become. These questions will need considerable time to ponder. It is helpful to write down your responses. Consider your responses in two categories, immediate and long-term.

For me, I know I'm at a place where I know this is the time for me. Due to life events, I've been too busy (caught up) to even appreciate all the things that matter. I hear others speaking about balance; it is impossible to achieve. While in the midst of living life (especially if you're in the fast lane, living large) it's impossible to live life in balance. So, stop the endless frustration and agony of the pursuit of living in balance. Maybe a more realistic challenge is to strive for moderation. Think about this for a moment: for those of you who know what a teeter-totter or seesaw" is, the next time you go to a park or playground, notice the position of this mechanical thing. One end up and the other end down—never both ends level, balanced. I prove my point.

Never regret a day in your life:

Good days give you Happiness
Bad days give you Experiences
Worst days give you Lessons
Best days give you Memories
Author Unknown

> ***Lesson in Resilience:*** If you walk through life carrying a hammer, eventually everything begins to look like a nail. Don't fixate on where you are headed, glance in the rearview mirror and look back at where you have been. Find that place where you lose track of time and at the end of the day, you are still energized. Live your "remainder" doing what you were created to do. In finding that sweet spot, you will gain resilience.

Refuse to Surrender

"Where there is no struggle, there is no strength."

—ANONYMOUS

I included this chapter for the sole purpose of illustrating effective ways to conquer challenges to help one gain resilience. Also, I will touch on a couple aspects of motivation and the associated parts of the mind. The premise: as humans, our primary goal is to survive—that is our primal instinctive nature that makes us want to thrive.

My determination must have started while I was in the womb. I was determined to not only survive but also thrive to reach a desired goal, refusing to surrender at all costs. Nothing gets stronger without resistance – Law of Exertion. Over the course of my life, I frequently endured situations that were insurmountable and impossible, but I was able to persevere until the end. Crunch Time, when losing is not an option. I learned this along the path of struggles. Through enduring each encounter, I built mental muscle, which enabled me to handle the next challenge. That mental muscle gave me a level of determination I call resilience. In his book, *The Road Less Traveled*, Scott Peck writes, "Yet it is in this whole process of meeting and solving problems that life has meaning. It is only

because of problems that we grow mentally and spiritually"
(2003). Resilient folks welcome the challenges and the pain
encountered while living life.

I learned early in life that when my body, mind, and soul
worked together, congruently, I accomplish more. This belief
runs parallel with the components of emotional intelligence,
utilizing innate talents, goal focus, and intention. When these
are aligned, we have a sense of increased, or even limitless,
potential. Emotional intelligence means understanding
which of your three brains is operating (reptilian, limbic, or
neocortex), and which brain[s] you need to be in. Emotions
guide us and give us information, but sometimes we need to
get to the neocortex to make the decision. For instance, you
may be angry and want to hit someone, but your "thinking
brain" will tell you this isn't a wise course of action. For
the same reason, you may love someone (limbic) while your
neocortex keeps giving you reasons not to (George and
Lorberbaum 2002).

Basically, the empowerment process works by calling
upon our emotions as a method of ensuring survival. It is
important to know emotions are more primitive and primal
than our mental process. Our decisions are connected to our
emotions. One study proved the hypotheses with the use
of fMRI (functional MRI); to detect the activation of the
various parts of the brain, a subject was asked an immediate
question, 97 percent of their emotional brain lit up, but only
3 percent of their rational brain was utilized. So, it is safe to
say we are emotional beings, and the majority of decisions
are emotionally driven (Šimić et al. 2021)

Pinker reports emotions are mechanisms that set the brain's highest-level goals. Emotions drive our reactions, which in turn are ruled by innate talent. Much of what a person learns happens outside of conscious awareness. Our Feelings are triggered by mechanisms that cannot be controlled. These mechanisms operate without any conscious or rational intervention. Emotions are required for superior performance in any occupation. Note: Emotional engagement is the fuel that drives the most productive employees and the most profitable customers (Šimić et al. 2021).

To understand the working elements of what causes our motivation levels and the activation of our will and intention, psychology has traditionally identified three components of the mind: cognition, affect, and conation. Cognition includes elements of working memory, judgment, and reasoning. Affects include basic feelings such as happiness and anger along with mental areas that allow emotional facial expressions. Conation is the striving component of motivation, the initiative-taking aspect of behavior. When utilizing the will, it gives us the ability to freely make choices of self-direction and self-regulation. Will is the cognitive process by which an individual decides and commits to a course of action or purpose-able striving. Volitional is a state of consciousness that gives us the ability to decide upon and initiate a course of action. It is simply the power of choice, the intentional or unintentional nature of an action. Conation gives us the freedom to make choices of self-direction and self-regulation. Some conative issues one faces daily: What are my intentions and goals? What are my plans and commitments (Huitt 1999).

In his 1992 article, "The Self-Regulation of Attitudes, Intentions, and Behavior," Richard Bagozzi says "Conation is the explanation of how knowledge and emotion are translated into behavior. It is the intentional and personal motivation of behavior" (1992). Conation is the self-regulation of attitudes, intentions, and behavior (Bandura 1997).

I haven't given up during my two years of recovery—or, better still, throughout my life—because I have refused to surrender because I was meant for more. I possessed the will to thrive, to be the best, to go beyond what is imaginable. Somewhere during my recovery or healing, my hair grew back (all my hair had fallen out), my skin cleared up, my body grew stronger, my laugh got smaller, and my focus returned to God.

I now start each day with prayer that includes the following: help me stay on course if I'm straying and encourage me to keep going if I start to give up. Amen.

Even though I've always known it never really applied to me, what is commonly known is how we underestimate the power and influence of our thoughts and words. Our thoughts and words shape us. Choose your thoughts and every word that comes out of your mouth, especially with the intent of how you say them. Always be vigilant when going to bed at night and when waking in the morning with awareness of your thoughts and what you are saying. At bedtime, it helps to write down positive things about your day and block anything negative about your day. This will ensure positive thoughts throughout the night, ensuring you will wake up the next morning with both positive thoughts and a positive outlook (Mayo Clinic Staff 2023).

We all have the power to surrender to a higher power, but it is important not to surrender to the negative worldly challenges and beliefs. Guard your heart and especially don't surrender to the negative energies that are constantly pulling, pushing, and taking us down with negative self-talk, and opinions of others. Pride is the enemy of peace and potential; one example occurred the summer of 1986—two ships collided in the Black Sea. All could have been saved, but almost 400 people drowned. Both captains refused to steer clear because of their pride (Eaton 1986). Pride is the root of all rebellion. Courage is mastery of fear, not absence of fear.

American explorers Lewis and Clark, while on their famous expedition, faced many incredible hardships. Many times, they wanted to turn back and not go any farther. Lewis and Clark, therefore, set short-term goals they knew they could conquer, thus helping them continue their arduous journey. Their goal—reach the Missouri River, knowing for certain the worst was behind them. When they reached the mighty Missouri, they knew the rest of their journey would be easy. While resting, they noticed what lay ahead, the Rockies— their biggest challenge thus far. They became filled with despair for a moment, then started climbing.

Later, they remarked that while climbing the Rockies, they gained the confidence needed for later challenges (History. com Editors 2023). We handle challenges in two ways: either give up and retreat or grow by developing the resiliency to handle it. Quitting is always simpler than enduring. Once quitting is started, it is a hard pattern to break. Diametrically opposed, the more you push through and conquer challenges, it becomes your norm. But at the same time, by keeping a cheerful outlook, you will in turn have more energy and will feel like taking on more challenges. A better mood, increased happiness, this is key to taking on challenges and you become more willing to endure rigors of life.

Obstacles are what you see when you lose sight of your goal.
HENRY FORD

Be strong and courageous. "Do not be afraid; do not be discouraged, for the Lord your God will be with you wherever you go"
(JOSHUA 1:9, NIV).

Lesson in Resilience: Strive for excellence not perfection. I find we want everything in life. But it is impossible to have everything, so it is important to decide what you want and go for it, making course corrections and adjustments along the way.

Conclusion: Aspirations Versus Realities

Following the survival of a heart transplant, which included several setbacks and recoveries, I can say with exuberant joy and complete certainty it is great to be vertical and breathing—completely alive! Not merely existing. Every minute, I am fully engaged with full-on gratitude for life and living. Go. See. Do. I am working on three things right now: myself, my life, and my peace. As of the writing of this book, I have celebrated two years posttransplant. I am grateful to report my test results are in the normal range, and I become stronger daily: mentally, emotionally, and physically.

I have known since childhood the importance of a good attitude and determination is 80 percent of the battle in any challenge. When embarking on the most difficult of times, when I am completely vulnerable, I find my most dignity. My journey is not special or unique and it is not filled with mystical or magical intrigue. It is a journey with true grit and transparent determination filled with faith, clear thought, and vision, with a full understanding of the power of thought and emotions coupled with the power of prayer and faith. I now live in a true peaceful reality.

I understand reality more now than ever before, I face life head-on, and accept the fact I have less runway in front of me than behind me. Since coming from underneath all the medical trauma, my soul is in a hurry. That reminds me of an analogy I once heard: "I am like a child given his own box of chocolates. He is eating them as fast as he can, until he realizes they are almost gone, then he starts to eat them with an incredibly special taste and appreciation for what's left."

My soul yearns for so much more, there are so many more things to go, see, and do before my last orbit around the sun. I now live with a vastly unique perspective of loving intensity that only this type of journey and maturity can offer. Since being spared from death, I am living an extension of my life, given a new lease on life to make every moment the best moment yet.

Since receiving this wonderful extension to my life, I have the opportunity to create a life with a new direction and completely new outlook. I fill my life now with people who are loving and giving. People who are curious, innocent, and nonjudgmental. People who can laugh at themselves are successful and know their calling. These people know how to stay in their lane and how to shoulder responsibility and stand in truth and justice.

I now find myself striving to quench an unquenchable thirst—I eagerly check my phone for emails, texts, and missed calls, anxiously anticipating "the answer to everything" message. Yet, in my head and in my heart, I know this call will never come. I am coming to grips that while on earth I will not know the reason for my extension on life until I cross over into the next dimension. Until then, I will continue to strive for contentment by doing things that add to the greater good. So live your life to the fullest. Make life your life. Write your own chapters; don't let someone else write them. Make them your chapters for your book—it's your life, live it.

I will continue to surround myself with folks whose hearts shine brighter after surviving life's trials and tribulations thrown in their paths but who still touch the hearts of every human they encounter. My goal is to reach the end of the runway in harmony with myself and my loved ones, with my conscience and dignity intact.

I now experience a heightened awareness of embracing gratitude and appreciation of every breath and every relationship. Appreciation is more about perceived value that is placed on something, it is more of a cognitive act. Gratitude is more showing of thankfulness. This will have a ripple effect on people around you. You think it, feel it, and then show it. I have learned the power of positivity and the power of words. I learned firsthand to choose words carefully as they will control (have power over) your destiny.

Yes, as we already know, life is short, with only a brief time to explore, to learn, to experience, and then create. It is essential we be fully engaged with the time left to burn brightly to leave behind a glow that will shine forever and will be an inspiration for those who follow the path. The path of resilience. Live every moment as if it is your last moment on this earth. Go out with a smile with no regrets! Keeping looking up and ahead!

To Become Better
Who do you have to become to be a better father
Who do you have to become to be a better wife/
husband/partner
Who do you have to become to be a better friend
Who do you have to become to be a better in shape
Who do you have to become to be a better salesperson
Who do you have to become to be a better leader

Are you struggling with self-doubt? Find your confidence by finding hope and having faith. Now that we are at the end of the book, I hope you have changed at least your perspective from when you started this book. R2S = Refuse to Surrender

Joshua 1:9 Be strong and courageous (NLV) He can steer the boat, but he can't make you row.

Don't live out of your memory. Live out of your imagination—what is possible!

Lessons in Resilience Compilation

Introduction – *Lesson in Resilience:* My journey has given me many scars, both figuratively and literally. From the literal side, the scars created from the transplant surgery. Figuratively, all the emotional scars created from the trauma of life challenges. A scar is evidence of healing, which makes the area stronger than before.

Chapter 1 – *Lesson in Resilience:* Acknowledge your own reactions to uncertainty. One simple way to practice being emotionally unguarded (to build resilience) is to express to friends how much you value their friendship. Naturally, this would occur after spending time together and if you both desire to nurture the relationship and be able to express how much you admire, respect or how much you love this person. In a child, you can see resilience developing by how they can self-regulate, take healthy risks, willing to try again if they fail, take responsibility, and feel optimistic about outcomes.

Chapter 2 – *Lesson in Resilience:* Sensitivity is essential to basic human qualities that lends to the ability to feel things at a very visceral level. If sensitivity is acquired, attentional awareness is a natural tendency based on this ability of sensing heartfelt emotions, in turn building resilience.

Chapter 3 – *Lesson in Resilience:* Control your thoughts, control your emotions: you choose your thoughts; your emotions are not your thoughts. Become the victim or victor—make your thoughts positive—positive self-talk. It is important to realize that many people will come into our life for primarily a season and a few people for a lifetime. Gain resilience when you learn to thrive, despite intermittent struggles and uncertainty.

Chapter 4 – *Lesson in Resilience:* Remain open to new ideas that will expand your vast horizons. Always be open to seeking help from others when uncertain and unsure. The key is to master the challenge, and it's okay to ask for guidance or help.

Chapter 5 – *Lesson in Resilience:* The capacity to recover quickly from difficulties. Life is tough. If you are moving forward, you will have challenges—get used to it. Ride the big wave for as long as you can before reaching shore. Remember overcoming challenges produces resilience, gaining endurance makes it easier next time. Let that soak in.

Chapter 6 – *Lesson in Resilience:* Finding purpose or finding success? Success, a global term, is often overused and misused. The word has specific meaning that can only be defined by each orator used. Success is a term used to express completion at a higher level of performance, career accomplishment, and/ or financial gain and prosperity. Success is not usually a word associated in terms of medical recovery. When I initially started my recovery journey, I set a goal of returning to the same level of emotional and physical quality I had prior to June 28, 2021. Along the way, I have redefined and adjusted my definition of success. Am I considered a failure if I only achieve 80 percent of my goal? Sometimes, reality is harsh and adjusting outcomes is essential. It doesn't mean you're settling if you've done everything humanly possible. It just means your new reality at the time is your success. Embrace and keep moving forward, gain resilience.

Chapter 7 – *Lesson in Resilience:* While growing up, mother often said to me, "Patience is a virtue, a virtue you will never have." I hope mother got the word that during my heart journey, I gained and experienced much patience. Waiting, without impatience or anger, develops resilience.

Chapter 8 – *Lesson in Resilience:* I have failed many times during my life. I have always taken the difficult goals and challenges, always confronted my fears and shortcomings. This is when I gained the most resilience.

Chapter 9 – *Lesson in Resilience:* The toughest reality to accept is that nobody gets out alive—each one of us has an end date. Acceptance and a deep understanding of death and dying will free you of the burden of fear of the unknown and constant worry. Age comes to us all and if blessed, we grow old. Die with memories, not dreams.

Chapter 10 – *Lesson in Resilience:* The answer to getting through a heart transplant is resilience. First, diagnosis of heart failure is a substantial blow to a person's invincibility. Second, a positive outlook is a tremendous advantage to surviving and thriving. Third, learn the difference of being vulnerable, but realizing invincible. Remember, avoid negative thinking, trust in yourself, and seize opportunities that are in your reach.

Chapter 11 – *Lesson in Resilience:* I have learned during recovery that patience and endurance run in tandem. Patience in most things is a prerequisite; waiting for the right moment is essential. Endurance must persist through the challenges that arise along the way, not surrendering to circumstances. Ponder this for a moment: If you start today, imagine where you'll be next week, end of the month, and end of the year. If you don't start today, think where you'll be in a week, in a month, and in a year. Where you are versus where you could be. What are you waiting for? You can't buy more time—now what?

Chapter 12 – *Lesson in Resilience:* You have the power to create your future. Only you control your thoughts, feelings, and behaviors. Don't allow your negative emotions to rule your thoughts. Conceive and achieve, you are your thoughts.

Chapter 13 – *Lesson in Resilience:* Some are blind and can't see. Thomas Edison saw incandescent light before the first electric bulb ever glowed. It is important to have a clear vision that is filled with hope with goals in sight. Belief, filled with hope, gives one a clear vision. You must have hope to have a goal, and you must have a goal to have hope.

Chapter 14 – *Lesson in Resilience:* The body's capability to adapt to challenges, access stamina, find strength, and recover naturally is amazing. The ability to keep moving, even if it's a tiny step, especially when you are depressed or in terrible pain—this is physical resilience. Don't stop, don't give up, keep moving.

Chapter 15 – *Lesson in Resilience:* If you walk through life carrying a hammer, eventually everything begins to look like a nail. Don't fixate on where you are headed, glance in the rearview mirror and look back at where you have been. Find that place where you lose track of time and at the end of the day, you are still energized. Live your "remainder" doing what you were created to do. In finding that sweet spot, you will gain resilience.

Chapter 16 – *Lesson in Resilience:* Strive for excellence not perfection. I find that we want everything in life. But it is impossible to have everything, so it is important to decide what you want and go for it, making course corrections and adjustments along the way. Be strong and courageous. "Do not be afraid; do not be discouraged, for the Lord your God will be with you wherever you go" (Joshua 1:9, NIV).

ACKNOWLEDGMENTS

I first want to express my sincere gratitude and love to the donor and donor family. Without the pay-it-forward gift of the heart I received, I would not be here today, and this book would not have been possible. Thank you for the gift of life.

I want to give a shout out to Saint Luke's on the Plaza and my entire medical team: there are no better. I had total trust in you and the hospital. What a complete encompassing group of consummate professionals. Attention to my care, comfort, and survival is why I'm here today. All the doctors, nurse practitioners, nurses, CNAs—unsurpassed. From the bottom of my (new) heart. Thank you.

Ashley Bellchamber, Taia Bringus, my two daughters to whom I owe a debt of gratitude. They oversaw my medical care; no treatment was administered without them knowing in advance and without their approval. Love you both from the bottom of my heart, thank you. I knew I was in good hands without worry. They both made the journey bearable.

Gloria Benedict, what more can I say that I don't say to you daily—thank you for your undying support and reassurance. I will forever be indebted to you.

Joy O'Neill, thank you for stepping in and taking over the care of Aubrey. I can't even fathom how that would have played out in the end had she been left on her own. I am forever grateful.

Ron Finke, who watched over my affairs and stayed in close contact while on my journey. Much appreciated, trusted and generous soul.

Dennis White, thank you for the poem, taking me to doctor appointments, and mowing my yard several times.

Mike Copland, thank you for mowing my grass for the entire summer I was healing.

Scott Kisner, thank you for being a loving, giving brother. Thank you for watching over my house, Aubrey, and transporting me many times to and from doctor appointments, especially those times I was unable to walk and you carried me to the truck. You were there for many months, and you always responded at the drop of a hat. I will always be indebted.

Kristen Atwell, in-home physical therapist. Without your professional care, guidance, and dedication, I probably would still be in a wheelchair today. Thank you for giving me the determination that catapulted me to full recovery. You will always hold a special place in my heart.

A very special shout-out to all my friends and family who sent continual prayers and blessings. It lifted me and gave me security and hope to stay alive and recover. Many, many heartfelt thank you(s).

All my friends and associates who donated to the publication of this book:

Barbara and Ronald Williams
Barbara Edison
Bev Eimer
Bob Pohl
Bruce Appel
Candi and Greg Moore
Carl Anderson
Christy and Gary Kuzmich
Clinton Wynn
Cynthia and Mark Miltenberger
Dawn and Joe Gentle
Dennis White
Doug Wikoff
Dr. Garrett Griffin
Dr. Joseph Paight
Eric Koester
Eva and Ken Hillyard
Gloria Benedict
Hap Graff
Jimmy Myer
John and Susan Marquardt
John Pritchard
Joleen Hartman
Linda Denker
Lorna Farrell
Pam Epps
Pam Fulmer
Pamela King-Steele
Paul Eade

Ricky Goff
Robin and Rick Stroder
Ronald Finke
Sara and Bill Boos
Scott and Kim Osborne
Shelly Smith Fisher
William Mensendiek

APPENDIX

Chapter 1 – Life Begins with Uncertainties

Almond, Douglas, Kenneth Y. Chay, and David S. Lee. 2002. "Does Low Birth Weight Matter? Evidence from the US Population of Twin Births." Center for Labor Economics, Working Paper No. 53, September 2002. https://eml.berkeley.edu/~cle/wp/wp53.pdf.

Chapter 3 – Gaining Hope Amid Loss

WebMD Editorial Contributors. 2023. "What Is Hyperpyrexia?" WebMD. July 7, 2023. https://www.webmd.com/a-to-z-guides/what-is-hyperpyrexia.

Chapter 6 – The Harsh Jolt of Reality—Staying Alive

Cacioppo, J. T., J. H. Fowler, and N. A. Christakis. 2009. "Alone in the Crowd: The Structure and Spread of Loneliness in a Large Social Network." *Journal of Personality and Social Psychology* 97, no. 6 (December): 977–991. https://doi.org/10.1037/a0016076.

Chapter 7 – Throw in the Towel or Wait

American Society of Hematology. n.d. "Blood Basics." https://www.hematology.org/education/patients/blood-basics.

National Council on Aging. 2021. "Tips for Recovery after Being Hospitalized with Acute Illness." National Council on Aging.

November 08, 2021. https://www.ncoa.org/article/tips-for-recovering-after-being-hospitalized-with-acute-illness.

National Heart, Lung, and Blood Institute. 2022. "What to Expect with Blood Tests." National Institutes of Health. March 24, 2022. https://www.nhlbi.nih.gov/health/health-topics/topics/bdt/.

Chapter 8 – Fear of the Unknown

Aucoin, Monique and Sukriti Bhardwaj. 2016. "Generalized Anxiety Disorder and Hypoglycemia Symptoms Improved with Diet Modification." *Case Reports in Psychiatry* 2016 (July). https://doi.org/10.1155/2016/7165425.

Stanborough, Rebecca Joy, MFA. 2020. "Understanding and Overcoming Fear of the Unknown." Healthline (Blog). Healthline Media LLC. July 23, 2020. https://www.healthline.com/health/understanding-and-overcoming-fear-of-the-unknown.

Chapter 9 – Are You Prepared to Leave Well?

Coffin, Janis, Claire Gallion, Vishaal Motla, Nivan Lakshman, Pravin Vikram, and Richard Wang 2023. "How Advance Care Planning Benefits Doctors and Patients." Medical Economics. November 13, 2023. https://www.medicaleconomics.com/view/how-advance-care-planning-benefits-doctors-and-patients.

Planning My Way. n.d. "The Free Guide for Healthcare Decisions" Planningmyway.org. Accessed July 17, 2023. https://www.planningmyway.org/.

Sonia Sonia. 2023. "Prioritize Yourself: Liberating your mind from the Opinions of Others." LinkedIn. Oct 11, 2023. https://www.linkedin.com/pulse/prioritize-yourself-liberating-your-mind-from-opinions-sonia-sonia-yhlof/.

Ware, Bronnie. 2009. *The Top Five Regrets of the Dying: A Life Transformed by the Dearly Departing.* San Francisco: Hay House.

Chapter 10 – Heart Transplantation

Alshami, Ali M. 2019. "Pain: Is It All in the Brain or the Heart?" *Current Pain Headache Reports* 23, no. 88 (November). https://link.springer.com/article/10.1007/s11916-019-0827-4.

Awad, Marcos, Lawrence S. C. Czer, Margaret Hou, Sarah S. Golshani, Michael Goltche, Michele De Robertis, Michelle Kittleson, Jignesh Patel, Babak Azarbal, Evan Kransdorf, Fardad Esmailian, Alfredo Trento, and Jon A. Kobashigawa. 2016. "Early Denervation and Later Reinnervation of the Heart Following Cardiac Transplantation: A Review." *Journal of the American Heart Association* 5, no. 11 (November). https://doi.org/10.1161/JAHA.116.004070.

Inspector, Yoram, Ilan Kutz, and Daniel David,. 2004. "Another Person's Heart: Magical and Rational Thinking in the Psychological Adaptation to Heart Transplantation." *The Israel Journal of Psychiatry and Related Sciences* 41, no. 3 (February): 161–173. https://pubmed.ncbi.nlm.nih.gov/15754519/.

Mindworks Team. 2022. "What Is Deep Meditation?" *Explore*

Expert Meditation Advice & Insight (Blog). https://mindworks. org/blog/what-is-deep-meditation/.

Ransford, R., B. Gunson, D. Mayer, J. Neuberger, and E. Christensen. 2000. "Effect on Outcome of the Lengthening Waiting List for Liver *Transplantation.*" Gut 47 (September): 441–443. https:// gut.bmj.com/content/47/3/441.

Warren, Rick. 2020. "What Does Your Tongue Reveal About Your Heart?" June 21, 2020. Pastor Rick.com. https://pastorrick.com/ what-does-your-tongue-reveal-about-your-heart/.

Chapter 11 – Physical Challenges of Recovery

Bunzel, Brigitta and Kurt Laederach-Hofmann. 2000. "Solid Organ Transplantation: Are There Predictors for Posttransplant Noncompliance? A Literature Overview." Transplantation 70, no. 5 (September): 711–716. https://doi.org/10.1097/00007890-200009150-00001.

Lindberg, Catharina, Matilda Almgren, Annette Lennerling, and Anna Forsberg. 2020. "The Meaning of Surviving Three Years after a Heart Transplant—A Transition from Uncertainty to Acceptance through Adaptation." *International Journal of Environmental Research and Public Health* 17, no. 15 (July): 5434. https://doi.org/10.3390/ijerph17155434.

Martin, Corby K., Timothy S. Church, Angela M. Thompson, Conrad P. Earnest, and Steven N. Blair. 2009. "Exercise Dose and Quality of Life: A Randomized Controlled Trial." *Archives of Internal Medicine* 169, no. 3 (February): 269–278. https://doi. org/10.1001/archinternmed.2008.545.

Prescott, H. C., P. J. Posa, and R. Dantes. 2023. "The Centers for Disease Control and Prevention's Hospital Sepsis Program Core Elements." *Journal of the American Medical Association* 330, no. 17 (August): 1617–1618. https://doi.org/10.1001/jama.2023.16693.

Rosenberger, Emily M., Kristen R. Fox, Andrea F. DiMartini, and Mary Amanda Dew. 2012. "Psychosocial Factors and Quality-of-Life after Heart Transplantation and Mechanical Circulatory Support." *Current Opinion in Organ Transplantation* 17, no. 5 (October): 558–563. https://doi.org/10.1097/MOT.0b013e3283564f45.

Substance Abuse and Mental Health Services Administration (SAMHSA). 2012. "SAMHSA's Working Definition of Recovery." https://store.samhsa.gov/sites/default/files/pep12-recdef.pdf.

Chapter 12 – Emotional Toll of the Journey

Dunn, Susan. 2013. "10 Barriers to Clear Perception." Self-help Vision. https://www.selfhelpvision.com/mind/ten-barriers-to-clear-perception.aspx.

Neff, Kristin. 2012. "The Science of Self-Compassion" in *Compassion and Wisdom in Psychotherapy*, edited by Christopher Germer and Ronald D. Siegel, New York: Guilford Press. https://self-compassion.org/wp-content/uploads/publications/SC-Germer-Chapter.pdf.

Robinson, Lawrence, and Melinda Smith. 2023. "The Role of Uncertainty in Life." Help Guide.Org. Updated February 27,

2023. https://www.helpguide.org/articles/anxiety/dealing-with-uncertainty.htm.

Stanford Medicine. 2023. "Mental Health in Heart Transplant Patients." Stanford Health Care. Accessed October 11, 2023. https://stanfordhealthcare.org/medical-treatments/h/heart-transplant/what-to-expect/mental-health.html.

Chapter 13 – From a Caregiver Perspective—Living in the Trenches

RWJ Barnabas Health. n.d. "Newark Beth Israel Medical Center Heart Transplant Survival/Life Expectancy." Heart Transplant and Mechanical Circulatory Support Program. RWJ BarnabasHealth. Accessed October 23, 2023. https://www.rwjbh.org/newark-beth-israel-medical-center/treatment-care/heart-vascular-thoracic-care/programs-and-specialties/heart-transplantation-and-mechanical-circulatory/heart-transplant-survival-life-expectancy.

Chapter 14 – Importance of Good Physical Condition

Calland, J. Forrest, MD, Reid B. Adams, MD, Daniel K. Benjamin Jr., MD, MPH, Matthew J. O'Connor, BS, Vinay Chandrasekhara, BS, Stephanie Guerlain, PhD, and Rayford Scott Jones, MD. 2002. "Thirty-Day Postoperative Death Rate at an Academic Medical Center." *Annals of Surgery* 235, no. 5 (May): 690–698. https://doi.org/10.1097/00000658-200205000-00011.

Chowdhury, Madhuleena Roy. 2019. "The Positive Effects of Nature on Your Mental Wellbeing." PositivePsychology.com. March

11, 2019. https://positivepsychology.com/positive-effects-of-nature/.

Quint, Evelien E., Manoela Ferreira, Barbara C. van Munster, Gertrude Nieuwenhuijs-Moeke, Charlotte te Veld-Keyzer, Stephan J. L. Bakker, Coby Annema, Sunita Mathur, and Robert A. Pol. 2023. "Prehabilitation in Adult Solid Organ Transplant Candidates." *Current Transplantation Reports* 10, no. 2, (March): 70–82. https://doi: 10.1007/s40472-023-00395-4.

Chapter 15 – Discovering Life's Sweet Spot

Clouet, Benedicte and Alden Lai. 2022. "Global Study Reveals Most Workers Enjoy What They Do." Gallup (Blog). November 3, 2022. https://news.gallup.com/opinion/gallup/404495/global-study-reveals-workers-enjoy.aspx.

Komninos, Andreas. 2020. "Self-Actualization: Maslow's Hierarchy of Needs." Interaction Design Foundation – IxDF. March 25, 2020. https://www.interaction-design.org/literature/article/self-actualization-maslow-s-hierarchy-of-needs.

Rosenberger, Emily M., Kristen R. Fox, Andrea F. DiMartini, and Mary Amanda Dew. 2012. "Psychosocial Factors and Quality-of-Life after Heart Transplantation and Mechanical Circulatory Support." *Current Opinion in Organ Transplantation* 17, no. 5 (October): 558–563. https://doi: 10.1097/MOT.0b013e3283564f45.

US Bureau of Labor Statistics. 2023. "Employment Status of the Civilian Population by Sex and Age." US Bureau of Labor

Statistics. Accessed June 28, 2023. https://www.bls.gov/news.
release/empsit.t01.htm.

Chapter 16 – Refuse to Surrender

Bagozzi, Richard P. 1992. "The Self-Regulation of Attitudes, Intentions, and Behavior." *Social Psychology Quarterly* 55, no. 2 (June): 178–204. https://doi.org/10.2307/2786945.

Bandura, Albert. 1997. *Self-Efficacy: The Exercise of Control.* New York: W. H. Freeman and Company.

Eaton, William J. 1986. "Soviets Arrest Both Captains in Ship Disaster: Skippers Accused of Violating Safety Rules in Black Sea Collision." *Los Angeles Times,* September 5, 1986. https://www.latimes.com/archives/la-xpm-1986-09-05-mn-13475-story.html.

George, Mark S. and Jeffrey P. Lorberbaum. 2002. "Triune Brain." *Encyclopedia of the Human Brain.* Science Direct. https://www.sciencedirect.com/topics/neuroscience/triune-brain.

History.com Editors. 2023. "Lewis and Clark Expedition." History.com. Updated March 28, 2023. https://www.history.com/topics/19th-century/lewis-and-clark.

Huitt, W. 1999. "Conation as an Important Factor of Mind." *Educational Psychology Interactive.* Valdosta, GA: Valdosta State University. http://www.edpsycinteractive.org/topics/conation/conation.html.

Mayo Clinic Staff. 2023. "Positive Thinking: Stop Negative Self-Talk to Reduce Stress." Mayo Clinic. Accessed January 18, 2023. https://www.mayoclinic.org/healthy-lifestyle/stress-management/in-depth/positive-thinking/art-20043950.

Peck, M. Scott, MD. 2003. *The Road Less Traveled*. New York: Simon and Schuster.

Šimić, Goran, MladenkaTkalčić, Vana Vukić, Damir Mulc, Ena Španić, Marina Šagud, Francisco E. Olucha-Bordonau, Mario Vukšić, and Patric R. Hof. 2021. "Understanding Emotions: Origins and Roles of the Amygdala." Biomolecules 11, no. 6 (June): 823. https://doi.org/10.3390/biom11060823.